MICHAEL

About the Author

Richard Webster (New Zealand) travels around the world lecturing and conducting workshops on psychic subjects. He is the author of over a dozen books, including *Palm Reading for Beginners, Feng Shui for Beginners, Spirit Guides & Angel Guardians,* and most recently, *Candle Magic for Beginners.*

COMMUNICATING WITH ARCHANGEL

MICHAEL

FOR GUIDANCE & PROTECTION

Richard Webster

Llewellyn Publications
St. Paul, Minnesota

First Edition
Second Printing, 2005

Book design by Michael Maupin
Cover illustration ©2004, Neal Armstrong / Koralik & Associates
Cover design by Gavin Dayton Duffy

Library of Congress Cataloging-in-Publication Data
Webster, Richard, 1946 –
    Michael : communicating with the Archangel for guidance & protection / Richard Webster. — 1st ed.
        p. cm.
    Includes bibliographical references and index.
    ISBN 0-7387-0540-3
    1. Michael (Archangel) I. Title.

BT968.M5W43 2004
202'.15—dc22   2004048720

Llewellyn Publications
A Division of Llewellyn Worldwide, Ltd.
P.O. Box 64383, Dept. 0-7387-0540-3
St. Paul, MN 55164-0383, U.S.A.
www.llewellyn.com

Printed in the United States of America

Other Books by Richard Webster

For my brother
Gordon

Introduction

THE word "angel" comes from the Greek word *ange-los*, which means "messenger." Angels are considered to be messengers from God. They are spiritual beings with an important role to play in most religions. They are servants of God who exist to carry out his will (Tobit 12:18). Angels wait upon God, and serve him. Angels can be found in Judaism, Christianity, Hinduism, Islam, Zoroastrianism, and Tibetan Buddhism. There are more than three hundred direct mentions of angels in the Bible. John of Damascus wrote: "An angel, then, is an intelligent essence, in perpetual motion, with free will, incorporeal, ministering to God, having obtained by grace an immortal nature: and the Creator alone knows the form and limitation of its essence."[1]

Angels are always go-betweens between people and God, even though the descriptions and roles change slightly between various cultures. Buddhism, for example, has bod-hisattvas, who are considered angels, but are perfected people who postpone entering nirvana to help people who are currently alive. Emmanuel Swedenborg, the eighteenth-century visionary, shared this belief. The Hindu apsaras pass out joy and love. They also hold the dead close to their breasts while transporting them to the endless bliss that can be found in paradise.

Traditionally, it is believed that angels were created by God on the second day of Creation. The opening lines of Psalm 104 tend to bear this out in an overview of how God created the world. First there was light, followed by the heavens, angels, and only then the earth.

Angels are powerful beings. Because they are aware of this, the first words an angel says to a human in the Bible are "do not be afraid."[2] However, the fear never lasts long, as angels bring joy, comfort, and happiness to everyone who sees them. Angels are also intuitive, caring, and loving. Thomas Aquinas wrote: "Their will is by nature loving."

Angels are especially created for their task, and with only one known exception, have never been human. The prophet Enoch, author of the *Book of Enoch*, was taken to heaven by Michael, and transformed into the angel known as Metatron.

Angels are perfect spiritual beings whose purpose is to minister, help, protect and sustain everything in God's uni-verse. Everything, even a humble rock, or a cooling breeze, has an angelic intelligence behind it to ensure that God's will be done. Angels serve and praise God. In the Bible, angels are described as "ministering spirits, sent forth to minister for them who shall be heirs of salvation" (Hebrews 1:14).

In the Christian tradition, angels are considered sexless. In the Jewish tradition, angels are regarded as masculine. The biblical references to angels depict them as more masculine than feminine. The angel of the Lord who released Peter from his chains, and helped him escape from prison, appeared masculine in every way (Acts 12:7–11). During the Renaissance, artists made angels look increasingly feminine. However, John Milton (1608–1674) saw angels differently. In *Paradise Lost* his angels enjoyed sensual lives, including frequent lovemaking.

Angels exist solely to help us. Consequently, throughout the ages countless numbers of people have called on them for help in times of need. This aid is always freely given. As well as this, we have access to angelic love, power, wisdom, and support every day.

People have always argued about the existence of angels. Despite all the mentions of angels in the Bible, going back as far as Genesis, many Christians deny the existence of angels. There is even an account in the Bible of an argument in which the Sadducees declared that there were no angels, while the Pharisees insisted that there were (Acts 23:7–9).

Despite disagreements of this sort, there is a large amount of information about angels in the ancient religious texts of most traditions. A major source of information is the Dead Sea Scrolls, written by the Essenes, a religious sect who lived in Qumran, by the Dead Sea. Some authorities believe that Jesus was an Essene. The Essenes believed that they had to commune with angels regularly, preferably every morning and evening, to lead a good and balanced life.

One of the early Christian "bestsellers" was a small manuscript called *The Shepherd of Hermas,* which was hugely popular. The shepherd was actually Hermas' guardian angel. Hermas believed that we all have two angels: one who encourages us to do good, while the other tempts us toward evil. Anyone reading his book today would find it hard to understand why it was so popular, but the simple account of someone communing with his angel obviously struck a chord with the people of the time.

The oldest surviving depiction of an angel is on a six-thousand-year-old Sumerian stele that includes a winged figure pouring the water of life into a cup belonging to a king.[3] There are many representations of angels in the religious art of Assyria, Egypt, and Phoenicia. Remarkably, a Hittite depiction of an angel has even been found on the Gate of the Sun in Tiahuanacu, which appears to indicate early Hittite contact with South America.[4]

Despite these depictions of winged angels, most people sense, rather than see, angels. They appear in dreams, thoughts, visions, different weather formations, and sometimes even as animals or people. When Johann Tauler, a German Dominican priest and philosopher (c. 1300–1361), gave a sermon on the subject, he said: "They have neither hands nor feet, neither shape nor form nor matter; and what shall we say of a being which has none of these things, and which cannot be known by our senses? What they are is unknown to us . . . Therefore we speak of the works which they perform towards us, but not of their nature."[5]

Saint Thomas Aquinas (1225–1274), the medieval philosopher who was known as the "angelic doctor," believed that angels consisted of pure thought or intellect. They could assume physical bodies whenever they wished, but these were also made up of pure thought.

Emanuel Swedenborg believed that because angels were not made up of material substances, we can only see them when they briefly form a material body, or when we allow our inner, or spiritual, eye to open.

Of course, at the throne of God angels have no form whatsoever. They are called Thrones or Wheels because they consist of whirling balls of fire, or pure energy. This pure thought, or pure energy, is closely connected to intuition. It is possible that when you receive a sudden flash of inspiration, you are receiving a message from an angel.

Since the beginning of time, some people have been able to see angels. The Second Council of Nicaea (787 C.E.) expressed the view that "angels were not altogether incorporeal or invisible, but endowed with a thin ethereal or fiery body."[6] Many people see angels in terms of color. Dionysius, for instance, thought angels were like flecks of gold, silver or bronze, or red, white, yellow and green jewels.[7] Saint Hildegard believed that angels glowed like a red flame, or shone like a white star in the sky.[8] The seventeenth-century Protestant mystic, Jacob Boehme, thought that angels came in all the colors of "the flowers in the meadows."[9] His contemporary, Thomas Traherne, an English mystic, thought that angels were like glittering and sparkling jewels.[10] Emmanuel Sweden-borg felt the more important angels were the color of flame, while the others were red, green, and blue.[11] Charles Baude-laire, the nineteenth-century poet, dressed his angels in gold, purple, and hyacinth robes.[12]

Angels were first credited with serving God at the time of the Persian prophet, Zoroaster, some three and a half thousand years ago. He taught that angels and demons were opposing forces, and also came up with the concept of heaven and hell, which has had such a major influence on all later religious thought.

Babylonian prophet Mani, founder of Manichaeism, taught that good people would meet their personal angel after death, and be guided into the next world. This angel was believed to be the person's perfect self, and was closely associated with the good acts that the person had per-formed during his or her lifetime. This ideal, perfect self could only be seen after death, once the physical body had been discarded. Not surprisingly, Mani referred to the per-sonal angel as *al-Taum*, "the Twin."[13]

In 325 C.E. the First Ecumenical Council acknowledged the existence of angels, though this was withdrawn twenty years later when the Second Council stated that belief in angels hindered people from worshipping Christ. It was not until 787 C.E. that the Seventh Ecumenical Synod resolved the argument by stating that the Christian Church believed angels were created to intercede between man and God.

This Synod also endorsed the hierarchy of angels created by Dionysius Areopagite three hundred years earlier. Dionysius Areopagite was a pseudonym, and consequently, he is frequently known as Pseudo-Dionysius. There is a brief mention of a real Dionysius Areopagite in the Bible (Acts 17:34), and although he was originally credited as the author, the books of Dionysius Areopagite were actually written by a Greek writer in the fifth or sixth century C.E. Dionysius Areopagite invented the word "hierarchy" to describe the different levels of angels.[14] Dionysius placed all the angels into nine choirs, which were spread amongst three triads. The first triad comprised the seraphim, cherubim and thrones. These were the angels who were closest to God. The second triad was made up of dominions, virtues, and powers. The third triad contained the principalities, archangels, and angels.

A German mystic and abbess, Saint Hildegard of Bingen (1098–1179), wrote extensively on a wide variety of religious subjects, including angels. She agreed with Dionysius on the hierarchy of angels, but believed that they were arranged in concentric circles, allowing each triad, or group, to relate more easily with the other triads. Hildegard believed in guardian angels, but felt they supported only people who feared and loved God.[15]

In Elizabethan times, the famous astrologer and occultist, John Dee (1527–1608), claimed to have communicated with the angelic world and transcribed their secret language. Parts of this Enochian language were adopted by the Hermetic Order of the Golden Dawn in the late nineteenth century, and it is still being used in ceremonial magic today. The elegance and beauty, as well as the perfect syntax and grammar, of the Enochian language, leave no doubts that this is a genuine spiritual communication, and it is probably the most outstanding example of this sort of communication ever received from the other side.[16]

The most famous person in the history of Angelology is Emmanuel Swedenborg (1688–1772), a Swedish scientist who wrote extensively on the subject. Because of his scientific credentials, Swedenborg was taken seriously when he claimed to have visited heaven and communicated with angels. He believed that angels were invisible to most people because they did not reflect the sun's rays. However, people could learn to see them if they developed their intuition. Swedenborg's writings had a major influence on the work of William Blake and Rudolph Steiner.

William Blake (1757–1827) was a visionary poet and artist who incorporated many of Swedenborg's ideas in his work. He liked Swedenborg's concept that we are already in heaven, surrounded by angels, but are simply not aware of the fact. However, he felt that Swedenborg's focus on the goodness of angels was unrealistic, as it neglected the concept of evil. To him, both heaven and hell were necessary because they complemented each other.

Rudolf Steiner (1861–1925), the Austrian philosopher and founder of the Anthroposophical Society, began communicating clairvoyantly with the angelic kingdom at the age of eight, and eventually wrote a number of books on the subject. He believed that we are all protected by guardian angels who are most evident in childhood, but take a step backward to allow us to develop as individuals during adulthood. However, we can still call on them whenever we wish. He divided the angelic realm into three groups: angels, archangels, and archai. The angels were ruled by the Water element and focused on individuals. Archangels were ruled by Fire and worked mainly with groups, or races, of people. The archai, or universal spirits, oversee the entire human race. Rudolf Steiner believed that Michael, the subject of this book, had been promoted to the level of archai to enable him to help humanity as a whole.[17]

Between the time of Swedenborg and Rudolf Steiner, a momentous angelic encounter occurred in the United States. On September 21, 1823, an angel called Moroni appeared to a young man called Joseph Smith. Moroni told him to go to a hill in New York state where he would find a number of gold plates that contained the Book of Mormon. Moroni was persistent, and appeared to Joseph Smith three times that night, and again the next day. Joseph Smith found the plates but was unable to remove them. Moroni appeared again and told him that the time was not yet right for Joseph to translate them from Hebrew into English. He would not be able to begin for another four years. Joseph waited patiently, and after he had translated the plates, Moroni returned and took them back to heaven. However, Joseph Smith had learned everything he needed to know to start the Church of Jesus Christ of Latter-day Saints. Fittingly, a large statue of Moroni is on top of the Mormon Temple in Salt Lake City, Utah.

Over the last fifteen or twenty years, interest in angels has increased enormously. When Dr. Billy Graham's book, *Angels: God's Secret Agents,* was published in 1975, it was almost alone on the bookshelves.[18] Today there are hundreds of books on the subject, showing the steadily increasing interest that people have in the subject.

The archangels are the best known of all the angels. This is not surprising as their name comes from the Greek word *archein,* which means to be "at the top," or "to rule." Despite this, scholars, such as Dionysius Areopagite, frequently place the archangels well down in the ranks of angels. There is a reason for this. The most important angels were considered to be the ones closest to God, while the least important were believed to be closer to people.

If Dionysius Areopagite is correct, how is it possible for the archangels, second to last in his hierarchy, to be "at the top," or "to rule"? The explanation is that in special circumstances or conditions, we can see angels and archangels, but our eyes are incapable of seeing any of the angels of the higher ranks.

In addition to this, Michael has always been considered captain of the host of the Lord, or in other words, the most important angel of all. It seems strange that Pseudo-Dionysius classified him in the second-to-lowest group of angels. This problem arose because originally there were only two groups: angels and archangels. However, over a period of several hundred years different scholars proposed different orders, until a number of hierarchies of angels had been created. Consequently, even though the archangels were in charge of the War in Heaven, and still lead the army against the forces of darkness, they belong to Dionysius' second-to-lowest group.

Archangels fare better in the Greek Testament of Levi, which is part of a longer manuscript called the Testaments of the Twelve Patriarchs. In Levi's account, both God and the archangels dwell in the highest heaven.[19]

In the book of Revelation 8:2, we read: "And I saw the seven angels which stand before God." These are believed to be archangels, and traditionally there are seven of them. In Judaism, the first, or top, rank of angels consists of the angels of the presence, or archangels. Again, there are usually four or seven of them.[20] In the First Book of Enoch they are listed as: Raphael, Uriel, Michael, Gabriel, Saraqâêl, Remiel, and Raguel.[21] The Third Book of Enoch proposes a different list: Michael, Gabriel, Satqiel, Sahaqiel, Baradiel, Baraqiel, and Sidriel. In the First Book of Enoch, Michael, Raphael, Gabriel and Phanuel are called "angels of the presence."[22] By far the best-known list is that of Dionysius: Michael, Gabriel, Raphael, Uriel, Chamuel, Zadkiel, and Jophiel. In the Book of Tobit 12:15, Raphael says that he is "one of the seven holy angels who present the prayers of the saints and enter into the presence of the glory of the Holy One." In Islam only four archangels are recognized: Michael, Gabriel, Israfel, and Azrael. Michael and Gabriel are both mentioned by name in the Koran. In Islam, Michael controls the forces of nature, Gabriel takes messages from Allah to Mohammed, Azrael is the angel of death, and Israfel will sound the trumpet for the Last Judgment.

Nowadays, the Christian church accepts only Michael, Gabriel and Raphael. Uriel is excluded because he is not mentioned in the Bible. However, he is mentioned in the

Book of Enoch and other noncanonical writings. It is interesting to note that Michael and Gabriel appear in every list. The earliest references to archangels are probably in the Persian Amesha Spentas, although it is possible the astral deities of ancient Babylonia were earlier.[23] However, the fact that different traditions list different numbers of archangels tends to indicate that there was no "direct borrowing."[24]

The task of the archangels is to care for the other angels and to assist humanity. They exist to help you, and will respond to your call whenever you ask. You can ask them to help others as well. Each archangel has a specific purpose. Michael will protect you and give you courage. Raphael is the archangel of healing and wholeness. Gabriel will provide you with guidance and the gift of prophecy. Uriel can grant you peace of mind, and will help you be of service to others.

The purpose of this book is to show you how you can enhance your life by calling on Archangel Michael, the oldest and greatest of the archangels, for support and assistance whenever you need it. It will also help you find the "Michael" inside yourself. We will start by learning more about Michael in the first chapter.

One

WHO IS MICHAEL?

"St. Michael, the Archangel,
Defend us in battle,
Keep us safe from the wickedness and snares of the devil,
May God restrain him, we humbly pray,
And do thou, O Prince of the Heavenly Host,
By the power of God, cast Satan into Hell,
And all the evil spirits who roam around the world seeking
the ruin of souls.
Amen."

—Pope Leo XIII (1810–1903)

FIRST of all, we should find out who Michael is. After all, he is considered the greatest of all angels in the Christian, Jewish, and Islamic traditions. In all three traditions, Michael works ceaselessly to create a world of peace and harmony. He is the patron and protector of those who seek to have God in their lives. Michael is the only archangel mentioned by name in the religious texts of Judaism and Islam, as well as in the Bible.

The name "Michael" has been interpreted in many ways. It can mean "who is like God," "who is like God?" "who is as God," or "who is like unto the Lord." All of these names reveal the importance of Michael. In the Bible he is called "one of the chief princes" (Daniel 10:13) and "the great prince" (Daniel 12:1).

Michael is generally shown with a sword, but is also sometimes depicted holding the scales of justice, or bearing a blue flame of protection. Often the blue flame surrounds the sword. Renaissance paintings show him wearing armor. These symbols provide the key words for Michael: courage and strength, truth and integrity, and protection. He also provides sympathy, patience, motivation, and ambition. You can call on him whenever you need help in these areas.

Using different names, Michael has helped humanity from the very beginning. He is known as Indra in the Indian Rig Veda, Vahman in the Persian Denkard, Marduk in the Babylonian Epic of Creation, and Apollo in Homer's Hymn to Apollo. He has also been associated with the ancient Egyptian god Anubis, who was the "weigher of souls."

Michael has been considered important since the time of the Chaldeans. It is thought that Michael was originally considered to be a protective spirit, or even a god, in ancient Chaldea. Their belief in the importance of angels, coupled with their need to have a figurehead in the continual battle between the forces of good and evil, helped raise the profile of Michael.

Michael was the obvious choice. Lucifer had refused to bow down and worship God, and as a result, Michael was asked to cast him and his followers out of heaven. The battle against the dragon and Lucifer can be found in the Book of Revelation 12:7–17. An old legend says that Michael chained the fallen angels in midair until the Day of Judgment. This is a fitting punishment, as they are able to see heaven above them and the earth below. They continually see the souls of human beings rising up to the heaven that they have lost forever.

God rewarded Michael by allowing him to receive the immortal souls as they entered heaven. He weighs them to balance their good and bad deeds (Psalms 62:9, Daniel 5:27). Those with more good deeds than bad were presented to God, while the others were sent to purgatory. Michael is also allowed to blow the trumpet and raise the banner on the Day of Judgment.

Michael in the Christian Tradition

According to the Gnostics, Michael was present at the creation of the universe. The Gnostics believe that the universe was created by the seven archangels, who were ranked next to God. When the world was divided up afterward, Michael was placed in charge of God's chosen people, the Israelites (Daniel 10:21, 12:1). In time, of course, Michael also became the prince of Christianity.

According to at least one account, Michael was involved in the creation of humankind. The apocryphal Gospel of Bartholomew tells how God created man from clay that Michael had obtained from the four corners of the earth.

In the Dead Sea Scrolls he is referred to as the Prince of Light, the warrior against darkness. Ever since defeating the forces of Satan, Michael has led the battle against evil. He is generally seen as the heavenly warrior who tirelessly fights the forces of evil. This is why, in the Middle Ages, he was considered the patron saint of knights.

In the Greek Apocalypse of Baruch, Michael lives in the fourth heaven. The fourth heaven is described as containing a large beautiful plain surrounding a magnificent lake. According to another text (The Apocalypse of Paul), Michael washes sinners after death in the white waters of the Acherusian Lake.[1] Many different species of birds that are not found on earth live here. In fact, they are not really birds at all, but souls who continuously praise and worship God.

Baruch reported that Michael was the gatekeeper to the Kingdom of Heaven, and no one could pass from the fourth to the fifth heaven until Michael opened the gate. Michael also carried an enormous bowl full of flowers, representing prayers from angels, which he took to God (Baruch 11:4). After visiting God, Michael returned with oil, which he gave to the angels. The quantity they received was determined by the quality and quantity of prayers they had offered (Baruch 15:2–4).

Baruch stood outside the gates to the fifth heaven, but was not invited in. As a result of this, he believed that no one could communicate with God, without using Michael as a mediator. However, although he failed to enter the fifth heaven himself, Baruch considered his visit a success as he had learned that God pays attention to people's prayers and allows the righteous to enter heaven.[2]

The Gospel of Nicodemus describes Christ's descent into hell, and the first resurrection of the just. People who have not previously been baptized, including the two narrators, are immersed by Michael in the River Jordan, and then go on to celebrate the Passover of the resurrection, followed by eternal bliss in heaven.[3]

Interestingly, Michael, despite never having been human, was sanctified by the Catholic Church and became St. Michael. This extraordinary occurrence was intended to bring Michael closer to humanity than the other angels. People became saints because they had endured great hardships and deprivation, even martyrdom, because of their faith, or because they had exhibited enormous piety and holiness. Of course, they also had to have healed others or performed miracles. Because of this, many people felt closer to saints than they did to angels. As a result, over a period of time, saints came to be considered more important than angels. Consequently, the Catholic Church effectively honored Michael by making him Saint Michael, and even today he is considered the mightiest of all saints.

In the apocryphal Book of Adam and Eve, Michael apparently kept a watchful eye on the couple, even after they were expelled from the Garden of Eden. He taught Adam how to farm, and even took him on a tour of heaven in a fiery chariot. When Adam died, Michael convinced God to allow Adam's soul to return to heaven and be cleansed of its sin.[4]

According to tradition, it was Michael who told Sarah, the wife of Abraham, that she would bear a son. Michael, Gabriel, and Raphael were on a mission for God and had temporarily taken on human form. Michael's task was to tell Sarah the happy news of her impending pregnancy, Raphael was to heal Abraham after his circumcision, and Gabriel was charged with destroying Sodom and Gomorrah. The three archangels are not mentioned by name in the Biblical account of this meeting (Genesis 18:2–33).

Michael is also credited with stopping Abraham from sacrificing his son, Isaac (Genesis 22:10). This was a test of Abraham's faith, and it must have been an enormous relief to hear Michael say: "Lay not thine hand upon the lad, neither do thou any thing unto him: for now I know that thou fearest God, seeing that thou hast not withheld thy son, thine only son from me." (Genesis 22:12)

In the Testament of Abraham, Michael took Abraham on a tour of the inhabited world. After Michael told him he was about to die, Abraham asked God for this tour, so that he could see all the wonderful things that God had created. He told God that he would die without regret or sorrow after he had seen all these wonders. After the tour he returned home and prepared to die.[5] Not surprisingly, after this experience, Michael became the angel who has the task of guiding departed souls to the next world.

As we have seen, Michael is mentioned frequently in the apocryphal texts. He is also referred to by name four times in the canonical Bible: Daniel 10, Daniel 12, Jude 9, and Revelation 12.

Michael was the angel who rescued Daniel from the lion's den (Daniel 6:22). The second half of the Book of Daniel describes his many visions, including a vision of a mighty angel (Daniel 10:5–21). In verse 13 of this chapter he is called "Michael, one of the chief princes." In Daniel 12:1, Daniel writes: "And at that time shall Michael stand up, the great prince which standeth for the children of thy people."

It was believed that Michael was responsible for the plagues on Egypt, and then led the Israelites to freedom.

The Jews, and also some of the early Christian fathers, believed that it was Michael, rather than God, who spoke to Moses from the burning bush, and also gave him the ten commandments on Mount Sinai.[6] Michael argued with Lucifer for the body of Moses (Jude, v. 9).

There are other biblical references that appear to refer to Michael. For instance, it was Michael who appeared to Joshua and called himself "captain of the host of the Lord" (Joshua 5:13–15). Michael also appeared to Gideon and gave him the courage to fight his foes (Judges 6:11–18).

According to legend, Michael was the guardian of Jesus and the Virgin Mary, charged with looking after them while they were on earth.[7] The legend also says that Jesus Christ asked Michael to advise his mother of her impending death, and to look after her soul when it crossed over.

This is why Michael is often known as the Christian angel of death. When someone is dying, Michael appears and gives each soul a chance to redeem itself, frustrating Satan and his helpers as a result.

St. Paul did not appear to approve of angels and told the Colossians not to worship them (Colossians 2:18). This is probably because of an apparition of Michael at Colossae, in Phrygia, that caused the people to particularly venerate him. The worship of angels was considered a heresy by the early church. However, they were not consistent with this. Emperor Constantine, for example, dedicated a church to Archangel Michael in Constantinople, and many miracles are believed to have occurred there as a result. At that time, Michael was more famous for his healing gifts than anything else, and many springs of healing waters were dedicated to him. Michael is believed to have appeared to Emperor Constantine at Sosthenion, some fifty miles south of Constantinople, and sick people began sleeping in the church there, hoping to see Michael.

Three important visions of Michael ensured his popularity in the West. The first of these occurred in southern Italy in 492 C.E. A wealthy man named Galgano (also known as Gargano) owned many cattle and sheep who fed on the side of a mountain. One day, a bull strayed and Galgano summoned his men to look for it. The bull was found at the entrance of a cave at the top of the mountain. Galgano was angry at the time, and his energy had been expended in finding the bull, so he asked one of his servants to kill it. The servant shot an arrow at the bull. However, miraculously, the arrow turned around in midair and went straight into the heart of the man who had sent it, killing him instantly.

Galgano and his servants were distressed with this, and asked a local bishop for advice. The bishop fasted and prayed for three days. At the end of this time, Michael appeared to him in a vision. In the vision, Michael descended to earth on the spot where the bull had been found and told the bishop that the man had been slain because the place was sacred to him, and that he wanted a church to be built there in his honor.

When the bishop brought Galgano and his colleagues to the cave, they found three altars inside, one of them covered with a beautifully embroidered crimson and gold altar cloth. A stream of pure water sprang out from a rock, and was discovered to have healing qualities.

Naturally, a church was erected on the site, and became a popular place of pilgrimage, as many people wanted to see where Michael had walked. This cave is known as the Celestial Basilica. Pilgrims still visit the cave today, and admire the magnificent works of art and the beautiful marble statue of Michael, carved by Sansovino. Michael is shown victorious after defeating a hideous monster.[8]

The cult of Michael gained popularity in the fourth century, and his appearance at Monte Galgano in 492 C.E. did much to help his reputation as God's champion. From the fourth century onward, he became the angel to pray to in times of crisis, especially at the moment of death.

There is a fourth-century Coptic manuscript that tells of Michael standing beside a dying man. Michael and Gabriel then look after the soul, once the man has died.[9]

Legend says that Emperor Henry II (973–1024), the last Saxon ruler of Germany, took a pilgrimage to the Celestial Basilica two years before his death, and was shut in the cave overnight. Michael, and a team of angels, appeared and performed a celestial liturgy for him. Henry II was named Holy Roman Emperor by Pope Benedict VIII in 1014, and was frequently known as the Saint, because of the way in which he managed to be a priestly king.

A second vision was even more remarkable and occurred a century later in Rome. At that time a plague had devastated the city. In an attempt to end the pestilence, St. Gregory, later to become pope, told the inhabitants to form a procession through the streets of the city. Gregory, himself, led the procession. For three days, the procession weaved its way through the streets of Rome, and finally reached the Tomb of Hadrian. Gregory saw Michael alight on top of the monument, and casually sheath a sword that was dripping with blood. Gregory instantly knew that the plague was over, and erected a church at the site which he dedicated to Michael. In more recent times, Pope Benedict XIV had a large bronze statue of Michael placed on Hadrian's tomb to commemorate this miraculous visitation.

The third vision involved Aubert, Bishop of Avranches, and occurred in 706 C.E. Just off the coast of Normandy is a large rock that turns into an island at high tide. Because of its isolation and inaccessibility, it had been used as a fortress and a prison. Aubert had a vision one night in which Michael came to him and told him to visit the highest point on the rock. He told Aubert that he would find a bull hidden there, and he was to build a church that covered the entire area that the bull had trampled with his hooves. He would also find a spring of healing water.

Aubert ignored the vision, thinking that it was just a dream. However, the vision occurred on two further occasions, and finally Michael touched his forehead with his thumb, leaving a mark that remained for the rest of the bishop's life. Naturally, after this experience, Aubert visited the site and built a small church there. This was later replaced with a more impressive church that was finished by William the Conqueror.

Although Aubert's visions were not as impressive as the earlier two, and in fact, could almost be seen as a copy of the first one, Mont Saint Michel became an important place for pilgrims to visit, and Michael was chosen as the patron saint of France. This grew to include England when William the Conqueror invaded Britain. Today there are few places that do not have churches dedicated to St. Michael.

At the time of the Crusades, the cult of Michael, the warrior saint, was used to help Christianize the Crusades, and this was also used to convert, sometimes violently, people in Nordic countries as well. Gradually, social values came to be considered more important than military ones, and the cult of the Virgin Mary started to take precedence over the cult of Michael.[10]

Joan of Arc (c. 1412–1431) began hearing, and eventually seeing, Saint Michael at the age of thirteen. He visited her in the form of a handsome young man, and was surrounded by other angels. He constantly encouraged her, and even suggested what flag she should use when leading her troops. He told her to follow the advice of Saint Catherine and Saint Margaret, and encouraged her to free France from English domination. At her trial, she told her judges that Michael had walked on the ground, but they did not believe her.[11]

At the end of the nineteenth century, Pope Leo XIII (1810–1903) fainted while at a meeting with his cardinals. Physicians who came to his aid thought he had died, as they could detect no sign of any pulse. However, a few minutes later, the elderly man opened his eyes and told the cardinals of a horrifying vision he had seen. While he was unconscious he had seen the incredible activity of the evil spirits who were working against the Church. Fortunately, Michael appeared in his vision, and sent Satan and his helpers back to hell. Shortly after this, Pope Leo wrote his famous prayer, which is at the start of this chapter, and decreed that it be recited at the end of mass to help protect the church. Although this was made optional in the 1960s, many people still gain comfort from reciting it.

Between 1961 and 1965, the Virgin Mary paid a number of visits to four children at the village of Garabandal in Spain. On the first visit, in October 1961, Mary told Conchita, one of the children, that she needed to change her way of life, attend church more frequently, and make a number of penances. Four years later, Archangel Michael visited the four children and repeated Mary's message. He also told them that if they prayed sincerely, they would receive whatever it was they asked for.[12]

Followers of the Jehovah's Witnesses believe that Jesus is actually Michael, and quote 1 Thessalonians 4:16 to support this: "For the Lord himself shall descend from heaven with a shout, with the voice of the archangel, and with the trump of God." As Michael is the only angel specifically called an archangel in the Bible (Jude 9), they have assumed that it is him. However, the passage states that the voice of an archangel will accompany Christ at his Second Coming. Consequently, it does not necessarily mean that Jesus is the archangel, or that this particular archangel is Michael. Further evidence of this can be found in Hebrews 1:6 where it says "let all the angels of God worship him (Jesus)." This means that Michael worships Jesus, which would not be the case if they were the same person.

Michael in the Judaic Tradition

In the Jewish tradition, Michael is seen as the keeper of the keys of heaven, and as the protector of Israel. In the Bahir, one of the oldest Kabbalah texts, Michael is considered the angel who is concerned with love, or the concept of giving without any thought or reward.[13]

Michael appeared to Moses in the burning bush (Exodus 3:2). There is an ancient Jewish legend that says that Michael, along with Gabriel, Raphael, Uriel, and Metatron, buried Moses, after fighting Satan for the body. This is also mentioned in the General Epistle of Jude, verse 9.

Michael can be aggravated as the old Jewish story of his confrontation with Jacob indicates. One day Jacob and his servants were about to move their sheep and camels over a ford in a river, when they came across another shepherd who was about to do the same. This shepherd suggested to Jacob that they help each other move the flocks over the river. Jacob agreed, on the condition that his sheep and camels crossed first. The shepherd agreed and his flock was quickly guided across the river. Then they started transferring the stranger's flock. But he appeared to have unlimited numbers of sheep. No matter how many were transferred across the river, an equal amount remained on the other side. After working hard all night long, Jacob lost patience and called the stranger a wizard. The shepherd touched the ground and a fire started. This did not impress Jacob, and the argument was about to turn into a fight when God appeared. The shepherd touched Jacob's inner thigh, and a wound appeared.

God looked disapprovingly at the shepherd. "Michael," he said, for the strange shepherd was indeed Archangel Michael. "Why did you harm My priest Jacob?"

Michael was aghast. "But I am your priest," he said.

God replied: "You are My priest in heaven, but Jacob is My priest on earth."

Michael felt embarrassed and humbled. He immediately summoned Archangel Raphael and asked him to cure Jacob. However, his difficulties were not over, as God insisted on knowing why he had harmed Jacob. Michael said that he did it to glorify God. God responded by making Michael the guardian angel of Jacob and his descendants for all time.[14] A brief account of this can be found in Genesis 32:24–30.

After their time of captivity, the Hebrews came to recognize Michael, the Spirit of Good, as the protector of the Hebrew nation. The veneration that the Jewish people have for Michael helped his influence to expand along with the growth of the Christian church.

Michael in the Islamic Tradition

In the Islamic tradition, Mika'il (Michael) is in control of the forces of nature, and has an army of angels to assist him. Only God knows how many angels are at Michael's command, and they help him send rain, snow, wind, or clouds whenever they are required.

Michael has a million tongues, each of which can speak a million languages. He has long saffron hair, which reaches to his feet. Each hair contains a million faces, and each of them contains a million eyes that cry seventy-thousand tears. Mika'il lives in the seventh heaven, and has glorious wings of green topaz. Mika'il takes his work seriously and never laughs. It is also believed that the cherubim were created from the tears that Mika'il shed when contemplating the sins of the faithful.[15]

God created a special house in paradise where the angels visit him five times a day for services, which are all led by Michael. Each angel sings and chants in a different language, asking God to extend his mercy on humankind. God rewards the angels for their devotion and praise, by providing mercy and forgiveness.[16]

Michael also looks after the Bell-Trees in paradise. These are golden trees covered with silver bells. The bells create such a beautiful sound that people on earth, if they could hear it, would instantly die, as the sound is so intense. Each bell emits a light that enables the inhabitants of paradise to see things that they could not even imagine while alive on earth.[17]

Michael and Saint George

Michael is also frequently identified with two other saints, Saint Peter and Saint George. He is associated with Saint Peter because they both hold the keys of heaven. Michael and Saint George both slew dragons, a well-known symbol of Satan.

In fact, Tabori, a ninth-century Arabic historian, related an exciting story that featured both Michael and St. George. His account was set in the Tigris Valley and tells the story of how Saint Michael rescued Saint George from the persecution of Emperor Diocletian. Apparently, the Roman emperor bound Saint George to a plank and had him scraped with iron combs. When this did not kill him, he was placed in a cauldron of boiling water. Again, Saint George emerged unscathed.

Diocletian then had him bound hand and foot, and placed a marble pillar on his back. This pillar was so heavy that twenty men were required to lift it. An angel visited Saint George at night and removed the pillar. Diocletian then had Saint George cut in half, and each half was further cut into seven pieces, which were thrown to lions. However, the lions refused to eat it. God caused the fourteen pieces to be made whole again. This infuriated Diocletian who had Saint George placed inside a hollow statue that was baked for three days. This time, Saint Michael broke the statue and rescued Saint George.

Diocletian became increasingly enraged at his unsuccessful attempts to force Saint George to renounce his Christian faith. Despite the continuing torture, Saint George remained staunch and resolute. Finally, God took pity on Saint George and received his soul into heaven.[18]

Courage and Strength

In 1950, Pope Pius XII proclaimed Michael to be the patron of policemen. This is an appropriate tribute to the archangel who is believed to have destroyed the hosts of Sennacherib and defeated the forces of Satan. In the Dead Sea Scrolls, he is reported as having led the angels of light in a battle against the angels of darkness, who were led by the demon Belial.

Monica, an acquaintance of mine, felt trapped in an abusive relationship. The cruelty was both verbal and physical. Monica blamed herself for the difficulties in the relationship, and managed to keep it quiet until she arrived at work one day with a black eye. A friend did not believe her story of walking into a door, and over lunch told her to ask Michael for the necessary strength to stand up for herself and leave the relationship. Fortunately, the friend was persistent, as Monica said she would, but then did nothing about it.

Finally, the situation got so bad that Monica asked Michael for help. As a result of this, she was finally able to stand up for herself. She left the relationship, much to the surprise of her partner, and moved to another city. She is now in a good, stable relationship and cannot believe that she had allowed the former relationship to last as long as it did. She now calls on Michael, and the other archangels, regularly.

Michael will provide you with courage whenever you need it, as he has an unlimited supply. In Revelation 12: 7–12 he is shown at the head of the army that will fight Satan, and bring an end to darkness.

In the process of giving us courage, Michael also eliminates negativity. We are often our own worst enemies, and Michael purifies the negativity from our hearts and minds, allowing us to make plans and carry on with our lives in a positive manner.

Truth and Integrity

Roger is a salesman at a carpet showroom. He performs his work with the help of Michael. At one time Roger used to do anything to get a sale. He frequently lied to his customers, but despite earning a good commission as a result, he felt constantly unclean and dirty. He was introduced to Michael at an angel workshop he and his wife attended. As a result of having Michael in his life, he decided to be honest and truthful at all times. In the past his integrity was constantly being questioned. Today, he earns a better living than ever before. He enjoys his work more and feels good about himself.

This is due to the power of Michael, champion of law, judgment, truth, and integrity. The Book of Daniel 10:21 says: "I will shew thee that which is noted in the scripture of truth; and there is none that holdeth with me in these things, but Michael your prince."

Michael is sympathetic and understanding, which is also why he is sometimes known as the angel of mercy. There is a legend that says the Cherubim were created from the tears Michael shed when he contemplated the sins of the faithful.

Protection

Sybil had to drive home through a bad neighborhood after a night out with a group of friends. She always felt nervous in this part of town, and only drove through it as it meant she would get home twenty minutes earlier. Just as she was saying to herself how she hoped her car would not break down, the engine died and the car slowly rolled to a halt.

Sybil locked all the doors and sat in the car wondering what to do. She remembered reading about Michael and how he would protect her. It seemed like a long shot, as she had never asked for assistance before, but she was prepared to try anything. Sybil mentally asked Michael to come to her aid. She felt a sudden peace come over her, and an awareness that she was not on her own. Finally, she was able to think clearly again. However, a small voice kept telling her to leave the car and seek help at a nearby house where there were lights on. Much to her surprise, she felt herself leave the safety of the car, walk across the street and ring the doorbell.

"I didn't feel afraid," she explained later. "I just knew that I was protected, and that nothing bad would happen to me."

She was right. The door was opened by a young man with spiked hair. Under normal circumstances, in this part of town, she would have been terrified of him, but she calmly explained to him what had happened, and he invited her in to phone for help. She called her brother, and while waiting for him to arrive, the young man made her a cup of tea while they discussed rap music.

"It's the strangest experience of my whole life," Sybil told me. "I felt safe, protected, and totally in control. Michael's aid transformed me. I've called on him several times since then, as I know he's always there for me."

There is an old Romanian story that shows that Michael not only protects but also defends people who need it. In this story, a group of wind-maids attacked a defenseless man who was almost blind. Michael tracked the wind-maids down and punished them.[19]

While I was writing this book, Michael helped two members of my family. My daughter, Charlotte, and her family were in the car, and about to back out the driveway, when Charlotte heard a voice telling her to look under the car. She did, and found the family cat, sound asleep almost under one of the wheels. If Charlotte had reversed, she would have run over her cat.

A more dramatic story involves my older son, Nigel. He was returning to his home in Ealing, London, late at night, when he was accosted by a man, wielding a large knife, who demanded money. Nigel was reaching for his wallet when he heard a voice tell him to run. He ran down the road, pursued by the knife-wielding man. Fortunately, the man tripped and fell, and Nigel was able to pound on someone's front door and yell at them to call the police. Before the occupants could do this, several police cars arrived. The man with the knife had stabbed someone fifteen minutes earlier, and the police were already searching for him.

In both instances, Charlotte and Nigel heard a small, quiet voice telling them what to do. They believe, as I do, that Michael was providing them with protection and advice.

Michael in Religious Art

Michael has appeared, both on his own and with the other archangels, in many works of art. The oldest example of this is believed to be a large mosaic in the Church of San Michele in Ravenna that dates back to about 545 C.E. This mosaic shows Christ holding a cross and an open book. Michael and Gabriel, with large wings and sceptres, stand on either side of him.[20]

Michael is usually depicted as an attractive young man, with a serious demeanor that befits someone who is constantly at war with the forces of evil. He is almost always shown with large wings. Early works show him wearing a white robe, and wings of many colors. From the sixteenth century on, he is usually shown wearing chain mail and carrying a sword, spear, and shield. Often, he is shown with a foot on Lucifer, either in half-human or dragon form, and his lance is raised ready to strike. This scene is popular because it reflects the triumph of our spiritual selves over our animal instincts.

Michaelmas

Dr. E. W. Bullinger, a biblical researcher, attempted to find the exact day of Jesus' birth, based on known facts, and came to an interesting conclusion. He believes that December 25 is the date of Jesus' conception, and that he was actually born on September 29. He also believes that the two greatest archangels, Gabriel and Michael, were involved. Gabriel appeared to Mary on December 25 to announce the conception, and Michael visited the shepherds on September 29.[21]

In the fifth century, the Romans created a holiday for Michael. Amazingly, the Feast of Michaelmas is celebrated on September 29 each year. During the Middle Ages, this feast became extremely important as Michael is the patron saint of knights. At one time the Catholic Church had individual feast days for Michael (September 29), Gabriel (March 24), and Raphael (October 24). However, nowadays the Catholic Church celebrates Saint Michael and All Angels at Michaelmas. The Greek, Armenian, Russian, and Coptic churches celebrate Michael on November 8.

In England, a goose was traditionally cooked at Michaelmas. This explains the old saying: "Eat a goose on Michaelmas, and you will not want for money for a year." In Ireland, a Michaelmas pie was prepared, and a ring would be placed in it. It was believed that the person who received the ring in his or her portion would get married soon. On the Isle of Skye, a procession was held, and people baked a cake, known as "St. Michael's bannock."

Michaelmas is also important for another reason. In Britain, September 29 was one of the four "quarter days" of the financial year, as their financial year starts on April 1. The quarter days were important occasions in which bills, rent, debts, and bonuses were paid.

Michaelmas also indicated the start of autumn, and marked a time to let go of anything that was no longer serving a purpose in your life. This included relationships that were not progressing, patterns of behavior, unwanted habits, and negative thoughts.

Now that we know who Michael is, and how he has been regarded throughout history, we can proceed to get to know him better in the next chapter.

Two

HOW TO CONTACT MICHAEL

A NGELS are willing to help you at any time you wish. All you need to do is ask. Naturally, you should not summon an archangel for a trivial matter, or for anything that you can resolve on your own. However, if the need is urgent, or requires angelic help, you must be able to contact a specific angel immediately.

Even though Michael is extremely busy, his presence is everywhere and he can come to your aid right away. There are a number of ways to do this.

Angelic Altar

It is a good idea to have a specific, sacred place that you use to contact Michael. A sacred space is any area that you use for spiritual work. The more you use it, the more sacred it will become, and the more effective it will be. In time, other people will be able to sense the special energies inside your area of sacred space.

Obviously, available space, amount of privacy required, and convenience all play a part in deciding where to have your altar. You can use any room in the house. The kitchen, for instance, may well be a good place as the hearth was traditionally considered the spiritual center of the home. Use your intuition, rather than logic, in choosing your sacred space. There is no reason why you should have only one altar, either. You can have as many as you wish.

If you are fortunate, you might be able to set up a permanent altar to honor Michael. Most people do not have this luxury, and use a suitable surface, such as a dining or coffee table, as a temporary altar. In some ways, this is not a bad thing, as a ritual can be made out of cleaning and setting up your altar each time you use it.

You can place anything that feels right to you on your altar. Some people like elaborately decorated altars, while others prefer a minimalist approach. You might want to decorate your altar with candles, crystals, essential oils, freshly cut flowers, feathers, and a few treasured possessions. If you have an angelic picture or ornament, you might want to use that as well.

You can change the items on your altar as often as you wish. Usually, this depends on the particular ritual you are going to perform. A friend of mine draws a mandala before performing any ritual, and places it in the center of her altar. The mandalas are only ever used once, and she keeps the old ones in a book that provides her with a highly illuminating picture of her emotional and spiritual growth.

Try to spend at least five minutes a day in front of your altar, even if you are not performing a ritual. You will find it energizing and uplifting, and at the same time, it will further consecrate your sacred space. Regular sessions of this sort allow your physical body to relax, which enables your soul to find its spiritual source. You will find this healing on many levels.

Invocation Ritual

An invocation is the act of invoking, or calling upon a spirit, angel, or deity for help or protection. We will be using this ritual to summon Michael, but it can be used for other purposes also.

You will need to be somewhere where you will not be interrupted or disturbed. You might like to perform this ritual in front of your altar. The ritual can be performed indoors or outdoors, depending on the weather and other circumstances. I have a special place outdoors, beside my oracle tree, that I use in the summer months when the weather is good.[1] At other times, I perform this ritual indoors. I am fortunate in that I have a designated sacred space in my home. If you have not set up a sacred space or altar in your home, you can perform this ritual in your livingroom or bedroom. Tidy the room before starting. Remove or cover anything that might be distracting.

Enjoy a leisurely bath or shower to cleanse yourself before the ritual. Some people like to fast and meditate beforehand, as well.

The best time to perform this ritual is when the moon is waxing. In fact, some people say that you should only ever do it at this time. I always check beforehand and prefer to perform this invocation when the moon is waxing. However, I feel that this ritual is so important that it should be performed at any time you feel the need for it.

Wear loose-fitting, comfortable clothes and ensure that the room is warm enough. You may choose to work skyclad (naked). If you wish, you can add atmosphere with incense, candles, and music. When asking for Michael's help, I usually burn an orange or gold candle, but prefer not to use incense or music. This is purely a personal choice on my part, and you should feel free to do whatever you consider necessary to create the right mood for the ritual.

The ritual takes place inside a circle that is approximately six feet in diameter. You can draw a suitable circle if you wish, or simply imagine that the circle is present. Stand in the center of the circle, facing East. Take three deep breaths and visualize yourself surrounded by pure, white light. Close your eyes and ask infinite wisdom for help and protection.

Touch your forehead with your right forefinger and say "Thou art." Move your forefinger in a straight line down to your chest area and say "the Kingdom." Touch your right shoulder and say "and the Power." Touch your left shoulder and say "and the Glory." Place both hands over your heart and say "for ever, and ever, Amen."

If you have worked with the Kabbalah you may prefer to perform the Kabbalistic Cross. To do this say "Ateh" (For thine) as you touch your forehead. Move your forefinger in a straight line down your body to the genital area and say "Malkuth" (is the Kingdom). Bring your forefinger up to

Raphael = East = Air - Yellow
Michael = South = Fire - red
Gabriel = West = Water - blue
Uriel = North = Earth - green

touch your right shoulder and say, "Ve Geburah" (the Power).
Say "Ve Gedulah" (and the Glory) as you touch your left
shoulder and "Le Olahm" (for ever, and ever, Amen) as you
place your hands over your heart.

4 great Archangel

Visualize that you are surrounded by the four great
archangels: Raphael in front of you, in the East, Michael to
the South, Gabriel to the West, and Uriel to the North.

design #

Open your eyes and extend your right hand, with your
arm outstretched in front of you at about the height of
your chest. Starting at the bottom left-hand side, with an
upstroke to the right, and in a continuous motion, draw a
pentagram, or five-pointed star, in the air. This is known as
the banishing pentagram. It cleanses and removes any negative energies or vibrations, while creating peace and harmony. It also provides protection. Visualize this pentagram
as a glowing, pulsing light. You might prefer to picture it as
if it was written in Fire. Once you have drawn the pentagram, point to the center of it with your arm outstretched
and forefinger extended. Say, "Archangel Raphael, great
Lord of the East and Prince of Air, welcome and thank
you." Draw a circle in the air, large enough to include the
pentagram.

The pentagram is a well-known symbol of protection,
and has been used in this way for thousands of years. Some
six thousand years ago, astronomers noticed that the movements of the planet Venus created the shape of a pentagram.
The point at the top of the pentagram symbolizes pure
spirit, and the other points depict the four elements of Fire,
Earth, Air, and Water. Because it is drawn in a continuous

line, the pentagram also represents the interconnectedness of everything in the universe. The circle around the pentagram symbolizes sacred space, and keeps evil energies away.

Once the pentagram has been drawn in the East, with your arm outstretched, turn to face the South. Again, draw a pentagram in the air. Point into the middle of it and say: "Archangel Michael, great Lord of the South and Prince of Fire, welcome and thank you." Draw a circle around the pentagram, and then, with your arm outstretched, turn to face the West.

Repeat the process, welcoming Gabriel as you point into the center of the pentagram. "Archangel Gabriel, great Lord of the West and Prince of Water, welcome and thank you." Inscribe a circle around the pentagram, and with arm outstretched, turn to face the North. This time welcome Uriel, after you have drawn the pentagram. "Archangel Uriel, great Lord of the North and Prince of Earth, welcome and thank you." Draw a circle to enclose this pentagram and then, with your arm still outstretched, turn to face the East again.

You have now formed a circle of protection and created a sacred space in which to work.

Close your eyes and extend your arms out in front of you, crossed at the elbows to create a symbolic cross. Visualize the four archangels surrounding you. You might see them as large, beautiful angels. You might prefer to visualize them as swirling balls of energy. You may see them as large colored lights: Raphael is yellow, Gabriel is blue, Michael is red, and Uriel is green. You might even see them with physical traits: Raphael with golden hair, wearing yellow and violet robes,

Gabriel with bronze hair, wearing blue and orange robes, Michael with hair like flame, wearing red and green robes, and Uriel with dark hair, wearing lemon, green, and black robes. Their wings are spread out to complete the circle of protection.

pray Say out loud: "In front of me is Archangel Raphael, while behind me is Archangel Gabriel. On my right is Archangel Michael, and on my left is Archangel Uriel. I have the Father above me, and the Mother below. Inside me dwells the universal life force. With all this help and protection, I can achieve anything."

Take a deep breath in, hold it for as long as you can, and then exhale slowly. Allow your physical body to gain a sense of what it feels like to be able to achieve anything, and then open your eyes.

You will find that although your sacred space will be the same, it will feel subtly different at the same time. It is possible, but unlikely, that you will be able to see the archangels. However, you will know, without a shadow of doubt, that they are there.

Lower your arms to your side and turn to face the South. It is now time to ask Michael for his help. Speak normally, just as if you were talking to a close friend. There is no need for ornate or old-fashioned language. Be aware that he is there, and is willing to help you in any way possible.

banishing pentagram At the end of the ritual, you need to retrace the pentagrams in the same order as before.

Facing the East, trace the banishing pentagram and say: "I now banish this circle. Thank you, Raphael, Archangel of

East and Air." With your arm extended, turn to face the South. Trace the banishing pentagram and say: "I now banish this circle. Thank you, Michael, Archangel of South and Fire. Thank you for all your blessings upon me." Keep your arm outstretched and turn to face the West. Trace the banishing pentagram and say: "I now banish this circle. Thank you, Gabriel, Archangel of West and Water." With your arm outstretched turn to face the North. Repeat the process, by inscribing the banishing pentagram. "I now banish this circle. Thank you, Uriel, Archangel of North and Earth."

Turn to face East. Bow slightly and say, "Thank you, Raphael." Repeat this in the other directions, saying "thank you" to each archangel.

The ritual is now over, and you can step out of the circle and carry on with your everyday life, confident that your request will be granted. You are likely to feel excited, happy, and full of ideas. Problems that might have seemed insurmountable before will now seem like minor challenges. Enjoy a few minutes of relaxation before returning fully to the material world. You might enjoy eating or drinking something, to help ground you again after the ritual.

Crystal Ritual

The powerful effects that crystals have on our physical, mental, and emotional selves have been known for thousands of years. Consequently, it is not surprising that certain crystals are associated with the angelic kingdom. The first person to do this is believed to be Pope Gregory, who considered the carbuncle to be a talismanic gem for the archangels.[2] Blue, yellow, and gold crystals relate best to Michael. However, use your intuition because any crystal that feels right for you will work. The crystals that I enjoy using with Michael are: sapphire, lapis lazuli, aquamarine, turquoise, and topaz (blue and yellow).

Sapphire purifies and restores the soul. It aids relaxation and meditation. It is known as the "philosopher's stone" because it enables people who wear it to find peace of mind and discover hidden truths. It provides energy, enthusiasm, common sense, and support.

Lapis lazuli aids spiritual development and enhances intuition, especially clairaudience. It removes fears, doubts, and worries, and promotes love and friendship.

Aquamarine enhances creativity and perception. It aids clarity, understanding, and perception. It is also sometimes used to strengthen the immune system.

Turquoise is frequently used as a protective amulet. It also provides confidence, energy, and enthusiasm. It cheers and brightens, while eliminating negative energies.

Blue topaz provides inspiration and helps release emotional problems. It enables people who wear it to look at things in a different way, and to express themselves creatively.

Yellow topaz enhances creativity and concentration. It encourages people who wear it to develop their spirituality. It also creates harmony and peace of mind.

Rutilated quartz is another crystal that can be used when contacting the angelic kingdom. It is sometimes called "angel hair" because the gold and silver rutile inclusions inside the clear quartz look like trapped hair. Rutilated quartz provides contentment, harmony, and peace of mind. It also stimulates spiritual growth.

Sit down comfortably in a place where you will not be interrupted. Make sure that you are wearing loose-fitting clothes and are reasonably warm. Place your crystal in the palm of your left hand, and rest the back of this hand on the palm of your right hand. Hold your hands either on your lap or at about the height of your navel.

Close your eyes and take several slow, deep breaths. Once you have done this, think about the crystal resting on your left hand. See what energies and thoughts come to you. You may feel the crystal respond to your attention. You might feel some of the qualities that the crystal provides spreading through your entire body.

Take your time doing this. If you perform the ritual too quickly you are likely to miss out on some valuable insights that occur to you during the meditation. When you feel ready, ask Michael to join you. Again, be patient, and allow as much time as necessary. Sit quietly, with your eyes closed, and wait for some sign that Michael has arrived. You might feel a slight change in the temperature. You might experience a sense of knowing that he is there. This can happen in a fraction of a second. One moment he is not with you, and in the next moment you suddenly realize that he is there.

Once Michael has arrived, you can mentally ask him anything you wish. When the conversation is over, thank him, take a few deep breaths and open your eyes.

Pendulum Ritual

A pendulum is a small weight attached to a thread or chain. My mother always used her wedding ring as the weight, and attached it to a short length of cotton. Specially made pendulums can be bought from any New Age store, but effective pendulums can also be made from any small objects that can be suspended from string or thread. The ideal weight is about three ounces. You will have to experiment to determine the best length of thread for you. Somewhere between three and six inches should work well.

If you are right-handed, hold the thread between the thumb and first finger of your right hand, rest your elbow on the surface of your altar, and suspend the weight an inch or so above the surface. If you are left-handed, you will probably find it easier to use a pendulum with your left hand. However, experiment, as many people prefer to use a pendulum with their less dominant hand.

Stop the movement of the pendulum with your free hand. When it has stopped moving, ask your pendulum which movement indicates a "yes" response. You can ask this question mentally, or out loud. It might take a minute or two for the pendulum to respond the first time you try this. Once you become used to it, it will move instantly. You will find the pendulum moving in one of four directions to indicate "yes." It might swing away from you and back toward you. Alternatively, it might swing from side to side, or move in a circular manner, either clockwise or anti-clockwise.

Once the pendulum has given you a positive response, you can ask it for the three movements that indicate "no," "I don't know," and "I don't want to answer."

Test the movements with questions that you already know the answers to. You might, for instance, ask, "Am I male?" If you are, your pendulum should make a "yes" response. If you are female, it should say "no."

Like anything else, it takes practice to become skilled with the pendulum. However, it is a useful talent that you will be able to use in many ways.[3]

Once you have become familiar with the pendulum you can use it in a ritual to contact Michael. Sit in front of your altar, and consciously relax as much as possible. After a minute or two, pick up your pendulum and deliberately swing it in a clockwise direction for sixty seconds. Stop the movement of your pendulum, and then say out loud that you wish to speak with Michael. Think of your need to communicate with him, and then ask the pendulum if Michael is with you. Hopefully, the pendulum will give you a positive response and you can start asking Michael to help you. If the pendulum gives no response, it means that Michael is on his way. Wait a further sixty seconds, and then ask again.

Once Michael gives a positive response you can continue in one of two ways: You can continue asking Michael questions that will be answered through the pendulum, or you can put the pendulum aside and hear Michael's responses in your mind (clairaudiently).

Meditation Ritual

A meditation ritual is an extremely pleasant way of getting in touch with Michael. It is best to do this when you are not tired, as otherwise you may fall asleep before making contact.

Lie on your back, resting either on the floor or on a firm bed. Use a pillow, if necessary. Make sure that the room is warm enough, as you are likely to lose a degree or two of body heat during this ritual. Wear loose-fitting clothes, and cover yourself with a blanket if you feel you need it.

When you feel comfortable, close your eyes. Take a deep breath in, and exhale slowly. Allow a wave of relaxation to spread throughout your entire body. Continue to breathe slowly and deeply. After several breaths, bring your attention to your left foot, and allow it to relax completely. When you feel it has relaxed as much as possible, bring your attention slowly up your left leg, relaxing your calf muscles, knee, and thigh. Once your left leg is completely relaxed, relax your right leg in the same way.

Continue upward through your body, relaxing your abdomen, stomach, chest, and shoulders. Allow the relaxation to drift down your left arm, all the way to the tips of your fingers. Repeat with the right arm.

Now relax the muscles in your neck and face. By this time your entire body should be relaxed. Mentally scan your body to ensure that this is the case. Relax any areas that still contain a degree of tension. When you are certain that you are totally relaxed, think about the muscles around your eyes and ensure that they are as relaxed as possible.

Now, in this totally calm and relaxed state, think about Archangel Michael and ask him to come to you. Think about your need for him, and why you are asking for help.

Gradually, you will gain a sense that Michael is with you. It is likely to be a feeling, but you may get a clear picture of Michael in your mind. You might experience a sense of comfort or warmth. You may sense in every fiber of your being that Michael is with you.

Once you know that he is with you, thank him, and make your request.

Clairaudience Ritual

Clairaudience is the ability to hear things clairvoyantly. Some people are able to do this naturally, but anyone can learn to do it with practice. If you have a large seashell, you can experiment with this by holding it up to your ear and listening to the sounds of the ocean. Naturally, this is not what you actually hear, but it acts as an audible screen that works with your psychic hearing in the same way a crystal ball works with psychic sight.

With clairaudience, thoughts will appear in your mind. At first, you may doubt the messages you receive. After all, our minds are busy giving us messages all day long. How can we determine which ones are psychic, and which ones are our own thoughts? One method of developing this talent is to imagine you are having a conversation with someone you greatly admire. Ask this person a question, and then think about the answer. Repeat this several times. When you feel ready, ask another question, but make no attempt to provide an answer. Wait and see what comes to your mind. You will find your skill and proficiency at clairaudience will develop best when you cease analyzing it and simply allow it to occur.

Sit down in a comfortable chair, with pen and paper. You might find it helpful to wear some lapis lazuli, as this crystal enhances clarauudient abilities. Close your eyes and take several slow, deep breaths to relax your mind and body. Visualize yourself surrounded by a pure white light, and then ask Michael to join you. You can ask out loud, or mentally. I have performed this exercise in a room with other people present, and they had no idea that I was contacting Michael. Obviously, in this instance, I said nothing out loud.

Once you sense Michael is with you, you can ask him any questions you wish. Michael's answers will appear in your mind. Do not evaluate or think about the responses in any way. It is a good idea to write them down, so that you can think about them later.

When you have finished asking questions, thank Michael for his help and support. Spend several seconds focusing on your breathing. Become aware of your surroundings, and then open your eyes. Wait a minute or two before reading the answers you wrote down.

"Writing a Letter" Ritual

This method is similar to the clairaudience ritual. Start by writing a letter to Michael. Write it as if you were writing to a close friend. In effect, this is what Michael is. After all, Michael loves you and is prepared to help you in any way possible. Start by telling Michael what is going on in your life. Provide as much background as you think necessary. This is mainly to clarify everything in your own mind, and is an important part of the ritual. Tell Michael about the important people in your life, and then move on to your hopes and dreams. When you feel ready, make your request. Sign the letter, and place it in an envelope. Seal it and address it to Archangel Michael.

If possible, wait overnight before continuing with the ritual. You can carry on immediately, if the matter is urgent, but usually it is better to allow some hours to pass between writing the letter and sending it to Michael.

Make sure that you will not be interrupted. Sit down comfortably in front of your altar, light a candle if you wish, close your eyes, and surround yourself with white light. When you feel ready, ask Michael to join you. Once you sense his presence, open the envelope and read the letter out loud. When you have finished, fold the letter again and return it to the envelope. Sit quietly, and wait for Michael to respond.

The reply may come in a variety of ways. Usually, Michael will send you a message that you will receive clairaudiently. Alternatively, you may picture a letter arriving in your mind. In your mind's eye, see yourself receiving it, opening it, and reading it. Another possibility is that you experience a sense of knowing that everything will be all right. Although you do not receive a specific answer in this instance, you will experience a certainty in every part of your being that Michael will be working on your behalf to resolve the situation. Open your eyes, confident that the matter is being attended to.

You may sense nothing immediately. If this occurs, sit comfortably for a few minutes, and then gradually become aware of your surroundings and open your eyes. Carry on with your day, confident that Michael will provide you with an answer when he is ready. On these occasions, you may find that the situation resolves itself without any need for Michael to reply. He will have attended to the situation and created a satisfactory outcome for everyone concerned.

Praying to Michael

In a sense, all of the meditations in this chapter are a form of prayer. When someone makes a conscious effort to contact the divine forces, he or she is praying. Praying is an extremely effective method of spiritual communication that dates back to prehistoric times. It probably began when people started talking with the powers of nature in an effort to control, or at least negotiate, with them.

When I was a child I was told that saying a prayer always attracted the attention of an angel. I do not remember questioning this, and probably assumed this was my guardian angel. I have always found it comforting to believe that an angel will come to my aid whenever I pray for help.

You can send a prayer to Michael any time you wish. You do not need to kneel down beside your bed with your palms held together. You can pray while driving your car, having a shower, eating a meal, or doing anything else. A prayer is a communication, and can be done at any time.

You can pray silently or out loud. I prefer to pray out loud, as this seems to add strength to my prayers, but obviously there will be occasions when that is not possible. A neighbor of mine prays for the well-being of her children every morning when she drops them off at school. As there are other parents there, she does this silently.

You may wish to start your prayer with something familiar, such as the Lord's Prayer. However, this is not essential. The choice of words is entirely up to you. Speak from your heart and the correct words will come.

Many people believe that Michael is the author of the Psalm 85, and recite this to invoke him.[4] After reciting the last verse ("Righteousness shall go before him; and shall set us in the way of his steps.") inhale deeply, hold it for several seconds, and then exhale slowly. Wait until you sense that Michael is with you.

There are two key factors about prayer that are often overlooked. Once the prayer has been made, you have to leave it up to the universe to manifest. That is why many prayers end with "Thy will be done." This shows that the universe knows more about what is best for us than we do ourselves.

The other factor is gratitude. Once you receive whatever it is you asked for, you must give thanks. You would always thank someone who did something kind or generous for you. You must thank Michael, and the universe, in the same way.

Walking with Michael

I enjoy walking, and usually manage to walk for an hour or so most days. It gets me away from the phone and other distractions, and allows me to think about a variety of things, while gaining some exercise at the same time.

The first experience I had of walking with Michael was unplanned. I had been busy during the day, so I went out for a walk in the late evening, before going to bed.

After I had been walking for about twenty minutes, a message appeared in my mind, suggesting that I cross the road and take a different route home. It was not what I had intended to do, but I have learned to pay attention to any intuitive messages that arrive apparently from nowhere.

I crossed the road and turned right at the corner. As I did this, I became aware that someone was walking beside me. I could not see or hear anything, but knew instantly that Michael was walking along the road with me, providing me with protection and guidance.

I mentally thanked him, and we enjoyed a pleasant psychic conversation all the way home. Michael left me at my front door, and I went inside pondering what had happened.

The following day, I heard that two groups of teenagers had had a confrontation in the area I had been walking toward. If Michael had not suggested another route, I would have walked directly into it.

A few days later, I was again out walking at night. I was thinking about Michael and what he had done for me. I mentally sent out a message of appreciation and thanks. Immediately, I felt his presence again. I told him that I was grateful that he had reappeared, but that it was not necessary. Michael replied that he enjoyed walking with me, and that it was a good time for a conversation. I seem to recall that on that particular walk we discussed some karmic issues that I was trying to deal with.

I have enjoyed countless walks with Michael since then, and consider walking with Michael to be one of the most effective forms of meditation that it is possible to do. There are many reasons for this. You are away from home and all the normal distractions of everyday life. Walking is a mild and pleasant form of exercise that sends oxygen to the brain and creates feelings of well-being and contentment. You are out in the fresh air, with new and different sights, sounds, and smells. A well-known tramp in New Zealand used to say: "The world is my church, and life is my prayer."[5] Spending time outdoors makes this extremely real to me.

A meditation consists of reflection and contemplation. You do not need to sit in the lotus position to accomplish this. I find that a pleasant walk, away from normal distractions, makes the perfect opportunity to meditate.

As you know, you can call on Michael any time you wish. However, enjoying a walk with him turns the experience into a pleasant conversation, and you will be able to cover much more than you would in a more standard type of meditation.

Walk briskly for the first few minutes, and then slow down to a more regular pace. Take some deep breaths and enjoy the fresh air. After several minutes, start thinking about Michael. Send thoughts of love and thanks to him. Think of specific instances in which he has been able to help you. While you are thinking along these lines, you will probably become aware that Michael is walking beside you. If this occurs, mentally thank him for joining you, and then tell him what is on your mind. If he does not arrive while you are thinking about him, pause after a few minutes, and then ask him to join you.

There is no need to be concerned if Michael does not appear the first time you practice a walking meditation. Carry on with your walk, and experiment again later. It is important to remain relaxed. You are likely to be disappointed if you are tense and worried that Michael may not join you. The best attitude is to enjoy the walk, and not be overly concerned about whether or not Michael chooses to join you.

Rest assured that Michael will always join you if the matter is urgent. (However, the evocation ritual is the best one to use when you need instant help.)

Dream Communication with Michael

In the dream state you are much more receptive to angelic messages than when you are awake. This is because you are likely to overlook them amongst all the distractions of a busy day. This is why meditation is such a good way of making contact with the angelic kingdom, because you are deliberately relaxing your body and quieting your mind.

To contact Michael in your dreams, think about your need while lying in bed waiting for sleep. Ask Michael to give you the guidance and help that you require, and then allow yourself to fall asleep, aware that most of the time Michael will provide you with the answer when you wake up in the morning. Usually, the answer will be in your mind as soon as you awaken. At other times, it will appear in your mind when you least expect it as you go through your day. If no answer comes during the day, remain confident that Michael will be working on the matter for you. Repeat the exercise in bed the following night, and every other night, until your problem is resolved.

Evocation Ritual

An invocation is a request for someone or something to appear. For the purposes of this book it is Michael. Most of the time, an invocation will be all that is required. An evocation is used when the matter is urgent, and you need to summon Michael instantly. Hopefully, you will never need to do this, but it is included for the sake of completeness.

If possible, face East. However, as an evocation is an urgent request, you may not have time to determine which direction East is in. In this case, stand in the direction that you think is East. It will make no difference to the evocation if you are wrong.

Stand with your arms by your side, and with your head bowed. Close your eyes, and visualize yourself surrounded by the four archangels. Imagine a pure, white healing light coming downward and surrounding you and the archangels. Take three deep breaths, and turn ninety degrees to the right. You are now facing Michael. Open your eyes, and ask Michael to help you.

In the most urgent of cases, you can summon Michael in a second. All you need to do is say to yourself, "Michael, I need you. Please help me."

Giving Readings with Michael

If you are a psychic reader, you will find the quality of your readings will improve if you enlist the aid of Michael. Before starting the reading, imagine yourself surrounded by a pure white, protective light. Hold any implements, such as a crystal ball, tarot cards, ephemerides, or a pendulum, in your cupped hands, or alternatively have them on the table in front of you, and imagine them also surrounded by the white light.

Silently ask Michael to provide his protection on you and the person you are reading for. Ask him to allow the truth to come through, in an atmosphere of gentleness and love, so that everyone will benefit from the knowledge and insight that will come as a result of the reading.

When the reading is finished, remember to thank Michael once more for his help, advice, comfort, and protection.

Experiment with all of these methods. You are likely to find that you prefer one or two of the methods to the others. Everyone is different, and the methods that I prefer may not be the same ones that you find most effective.

Now that you know how to contact Michael whenever you wish, it is time to learn how to ask him for help and assistance, both for yourself and others. That is the subject of the next chapter.

Three

HOW TO REQUEST ASSISTANCE

MICHAEL is willing and able to help you in any way he can. Naturally, you should not bother him with minor requests. You can call on your guardian angel for these. There are three things you should consider when calling on Michael:

1. Your requests must harm no one. It is important that your requests be positive and for the good of everyone concerned.

2. You can ask Michael to help others. Whenever possible, ask these people for permission first. However, there may be times when you can not do this, and you will have to use your discretion.

3. Michael is prepared to help you in any way he can. However, he may not always be the right angel to

summon. If your request relates to a broken relationship, for instance, you might want to consider
calling on Raphael, rather than Michael.

Michael is concerned chiefly with protection, truth,
integrity, courage, and strength. If you are having difficulties in any of these areas, Michael is the angel to summon.

Protection

You have a right to feel safe and secure wherever you may
be. Unfortunately, like everyone else, you will sometimes
experience moments when you feel the need for protection.

The memory that comes instantly to my mind occurred
almost twenty years ago. One Sunday evening, I was walking up the main street of the city I live in. Members of a
fundamentalist church were having a service in the Town
Hall, and their meeting ended at about the time I walked
past. Some members of the congregation recognized me, as
I had been on television a few nights earlier talking about
psychic matters. They became angry when they saw me and
chased me up the street. I was terrified and ran away as fast
as I could. My pursuers were gaining on me, and I finally
thought to call on Michael. To my amazement, the men
immediately stopped chasing me, and returned to join the
other members of the congregation. I have no doubt in my
mind that it was Michael who stopped them from pursuing
me. It wasn't until much later that I realized how ironic it
was that I had called on Michael to protect me from people
who professed to be good Christians.

This shows that you can call on Michael in an emergency, and receive instant help. Fortunately, that is the only time I have had to do that. If it happens again, I'll call on Michael more quickly.

Michael will also provide protection in a variety of ways. If you are in an abusive relationship, for instance, call on Michael for emotional protection. One of my students told the class how she had been sexually abused by her stepfather. After several years of this, she asked Michael for protection. He not only gave her this; he also gave her the courage and strength to stand up to her abuser.

Michael can provide psychic protection, as well. If you are being subjected to psychic attack, call on Michael for protection. Another of my students told us how she was psychically attacked by a man who wanted her job.

"He was always pleasant to me in person," she recalled. "But there was something about his eyes that worried me. They seemed to look right inside me. I even knew when he was behind me, because those eyes seemed to bore right into me. Until I met him, I hadn't really believed there was such a thing as the evil eye, but he certainly taught me all about it. Anyway, he was no match for Michael. He found himself another job soon after I called on Michael. I discovered later from someone who had lived with him that he had problems with many people, and dabbled in black magic to get even."

Naturally, you can call on Michael for physical protection as well. Several years ago I became lost in Niteroi, a city across the harbor from Rio de Janeiro. I found myself in a rather seedy part of town, and was concerned about finding my way back to my hotel, as I spoke no Portuguese. I called on Michael to protect me as I wandered through the streets, until I finally found myself in a place that I recognized. I would probably have been fine without Michael's protection, but I felt much happier with it.

I know several people who have called on Michael's protection in similar situations. A lady I know was travelling home late one night, and her car broke down in a bad part of town. She asked Michael to protect her as she searched for a pay phone. Incidentally, as a direct result of this experience, she became the first person I ever knew who bought a cell phone.

A thirteen-year-old girl, the daughter of friends of ours, was left alone in her home one evening when her mother was taken to the hospital with appendicitis. She called on Michael to protect her, and was sleeping peacefully in her bed when her father arrived back home. She was able to sleep only because she had called on Michael to protect her.

Consequently, no matter what type of protection you need, Michael is ready and willing to provide it. All you need to do is ask for his help. You can make a ritual out of this if you have time. This is a good idea if you are asking for protection for yourself, family, loved ones, a community, country, or even the world.

Don't let anyone tell you that one person can not make a difference. Your regular sessions with Michael will have an effect. Incidentally, I rarely tell anyone outside my immediate family what I do in my sacred space. Most people would not understand, or would misinterpret my motives for request-ing protection for the special people in my life. I find it better to conduct my rituals, as and when I feel they are necessary, without mentioning them to anyone else.

There is no right or wrong way of asking Michael for pro-tection. Usually, I do it near the start of a ritual, once Michael has arrived. I start by asking for protection for myself. I visu-alize myself being surrounded by a pure, white light, much as if I was standing directly under a large spotlight on a stage. I then ask for protection for my friends and family, and visualize the white light expanding to encompass them all. If I feel certain people need extra protection I will specify them by name. I then ask for protection for the people I work with. After this, I go on to ask for protection for my community, country, and the world. As I think about each group of people, I visualize the circle of white light expand-ing to accommodate them all. Once I have taken this as far as I wish, I hold the image of the white light in my mind for as long as possible. Then I thank Michael sincerely for his willingness to protect everyone I hold dear. Usually, I finish the ritual at this point. However, if there are other matters I wish to discuss with Michael I will ensure that they are dealt with, before closing the ritual.

Naturally, you can not ask for protection in this way in a moment of crisis. In an instance of this sort, say, "Michael, I need you now. Help me!" This works, even if you have not contacted Michael in the past. However, it is a great deal easier to do, and you are more likely to do it, if you are in regular communication with him.

Immediate, Long-Lasting Protection

A traditional method of obtaining both immediate and long-lasting, general protection from Michael is to burn a red apple and laurel leaves in an open fire. After watching the flames for a minute or two, read Psalm 85 out loud. Place the ashes in a small red bag, and carry this with you until the immediate danger is over. Then, on a Tuesday night when the moon is waxing (increasing), sprinkle the ashes around the outside of your home.

Strength and Courage

Michael is also willing to give you all the courage you need to face any obstacle or challenge. No matter what sort of situation you find yourself within, Michael will give you the necessary courage and strength to deal with it.

Some years ago, Natalie, a former client of mine, found herself in a difficult situation at work. Her boss got his way by intimidating everyone, and did not hesitate to scream at the staff if they did not do what he wanted. Naturally, this created a highly stressful work environment.

Natalie began looking for a more pleasant job, but then decided to face up to her boss because the position had good prospects, and she was learning a great deal. For several days, she conducted a ritual in which she asked Michael for enough courage to stand up to her boss. She almost spoke to him about his aggressive, overbearing manner on a few occasions, but fear held her back.

Finally, she felt ready. She asked Michael to protect her, and marched into her boss's office. She sat down and told her boss everything that was on her mind; how everyone hated his bullying tactics and loud voice, his aggressiveness and intimidation. Her boss was stunned. No one had ever told him this before. Natalie thought he would be angry, and half-expected to be unemployed at the end of the conversation. Instead, after listening to her for several minutes in silence, tears came to his eyes, and he apologized for his behavior. He asked her to help him overcome his faults and become a better supervisor. It wasn't easy, but with her help, he gradually started behaving like a normal human being, and gave her a wonderful letter of recommendation when she left to start her own business.

Natalie credits Michael for the change in her boss. "If he hadn't given me the courage I needed to stand up to him, he would never have changed. I changed too. After that experience I've never let anyone put me down again, as I know that Michael is there to help me."

I have done a great deal of counseling over the years. Some years ago, a former pastor who had lost his faith came to see me. He gave up his parish, moved to another city, and started selling life insurance. He failed at this, and all the other jobs he attempted. He went downhill even more when his wife went off with a man she had been having an affair with, about the time the bank foreclosed on his mortgage. He was so despondent that he was on the verge of suicide.

In one of our sessions I happened to mention the archangels. He told me, that despite his loss of faith, he sometimes felt the presence of angels, and thought they were protecting him. This gave me the opening I needed. I suggested that he call on Michael and ask him for the necessary courage and strength to help him overcome his problems and start life over again.

Secretly, I doubted that he would do it. However, a week later, he arrived for his appointment looking neater and tidier than he had been on his previous appointments. He was still depressed, but had obviously made a great deal of progress since I had last seen him. With Michael's help, he began to move ahead. The last time I saw him he was in a new relationship, had regained his faith, and was working full-time with troubled teenagers. None of this would have happened if he had not called on Michael to give him the courage and strength he needed.

An old schoolfriend of mine had been constantly teased at school. He was ungainly, unathletic and painfully shy. In his twenties he took a series of confidence-building courses with little success. The major change in his life occurred when he was almost thirty. He met a girl who attracted him, but he was too shy to ask her out. I conducted a ritual with him that invoked Michael, asking him to provide my friend with the confidence, strength, and courage to ask her out. Having a girlfriend for the first time did wonders for his self-esteem. Once he discovered that he could call on Michael whenever necessary, he began pushing himself more and more, and today there is no trace of the shyness and introversion that held him back for so long.

Over the years I have counseled many people with addiction problems. In many cases, asking Michael to give them the strength and courage to overcome these difficulties made the difference between success and failure.

Michael can also help people with relationship problems. Sometimes he will counsel people to stay together and work through their difficulties. However, he will also encourage people to walk away from the relationship, if that is the best solution.

Luanne is an attractive woman in her early thirties. While still a teenager, she met a young man the same age as her, and a couple of years later they married. Two children quickly followed. Her husband had few skills, and the family lived precariously from one paycheck to the next. Her husband began drinking too much, and blaming everyone else for his problems. Finally, it became too much for Luanne, and she and the children left. Her husband pleaded with her to return home, and, rather reluctantly, they did. Everything was fine for a few months, and then the cycle began again. Luanne left and returned several times before asking Michael to give her the strength to stay away permanently. Her husband refused to accept the fact that the relationship was over, and threatened to kill himself, Luanne, and the children. Fortunately, Michael gave Luanne the strength to stand up for herself and the children. She refused to go back, and finally, when it was far too late, her husband realized what he had done.

While writing this chapter, I met someone who had asked Michael to help him in a job interview. Apparently, Millard felt incredibly nervous before interviews, and this failing had cost him interesting opportunities in the past. He was determined it would not happen again. Consequently, he asked Michael for the necessary courage and strength to handle the interview well. It worked even better than he expected, and Millard is now enjoying his new position, even though he is puzzled that he had not thought to ask Michael for help before.

You can ask Michael for courage and strength any time you need it. Naturally, it is better to ask for help ahead of time, but there may be occasions when you need instant help.

I had a situation like this when a dog ran out of a driveway and appeared to attack my car. I slowed down, but he vanished from sight, and I thought I had run him over. I got out and found the dog trapped under the car, crying piteously. I called on Michael for strength, and then lifted my side of the car off the ground, so the dog could get out. He ran off, apparently unhurt. I had heard of situations when people gained much more strength than they would have believed possible, but this is the only time I have experienced it myself. I have a bad back, but lifting the car in this situation caused me no problems at all. It's amazing what can be done with angelic help and protection.

In your special times in your sacred space, ask Michael to give you the strength and courage you require. You can do this even if you have no specific immediate need. Ask Michael to give you the strength and courage to stand up for yourself when necessary, and to be able to stand up for what is right and good. These feelings of courage will become part of your nature and you will feel more powerful, and more in control, in every type of situation.

Honesty and Integrity

Being true to yourself is an important part of leading a worthwhile, happy life. Any time you compromise your integrity, or are less than honest, you sabotage yourself and fail to reveal your true nature. Fortunately, Michael can help you with these challenges that affect everyone.

A relative of mine feared confrontation so much that she always agreed with other people, no matter what her true feelings on the matter were. As a result of this, her self-esteem was almost nonexistent, and she felt bad about herself all the time. Fortunately, she learned that with Michael's help she could express her true feelings.

The first time she was brave enough to stand up for herself was when her husband made a political comment at the dinner table. Normally, she would have said nothing, but on this occasion she disagreed, and quietly gave her reasons for her point of view. Her husband ridiculed what she said. In the past, she would have retreated to avoid an argument, but now she stood up for herself, and gave a convincing argument for her position. Her husband was so surprised that he stayed silent for the rest of the meal. From this small beginning, she gained confidence and began standing up for herself in situations that she would have avoided in the past. With the help of Michael, her life was gradually transformed.

When I left school I worked as a sales representative for a couple of years. One of the other sales reps, who I will call Don, told me of a problem he had that had been concerning him for some time. When he took over the territory, his predecessor introduced him to all the customers. At one hotel they stayed at, the receipt for accommodation they were given was several dollars more than they had actually paid. (This was thirty-five years ago, and several dollars was quite a substantial amount of money.) Don was told that this had been going on for years and was a common practice. When he submitted the receipt in his expenses, he would be reimbursed and could pocket the extra money. For the first few trips around his territory, Don submitted the invoice in his expenses, feeling guilty about it, but not sure what to do. If he told his superiors about it, he would be in trouble himself, and so would all his predecessors in the position. Don told me this story over a drink, and asked me what he should do.

"Who does it hurt?" I asked.

"The company we work for," he replied.

"Yes," I agreed. "What you are doing is morally and legally wrong, because you are stealing from the people who pay you. But tell me, who are you hurting even more?"

It took Don thirty seconds to answer. "Me," he said. "I feel ashamed of myself all the time. I've always been honest, and now, all of a sudden, I feel unclean." He downed his drink and shook my hand. "Thank you," he said. "I know what to do."

The following day, Don went to see the company accountant with a letter of apology and a check for the extra money he had received. Don expected to be fired, but the company appreciated his honesty, and a few months later he was promoted.

The reason I have related this story is because of what happened a few days after Don faced up to what he had been doing. He told me that he saw an angel while walking up to the front door of his house. It was eight or nine feet tall and was dressed in white. The angel nodded at Don and vanished. Don took this as a sign that he had been forgiven. At the time, neither of us knew enough about angels to hazard a guess as to who it was. I now think it must have been Michael.

I related this story at a talk I gave recently, and a young woman there told me a similar story that had happened to her. When she was at high school she saw one of her classmates stealing from a store. By not doing anything about it, she felt as guilty, as if she had committed the crime herself. She approached the girl involved, who threatened her with all sorts of dire consequences if she told anyone. As she walked to the schoolbus that afternoon, she saw a large angel standing beside the door of the bus. None of the other children appeared to notice it, and it stood looking at her for several seconds before disappearing. Until then, she had not known what to do. However, she took the angel as a sign that she had to be honest and tell the truth. She told the girl who had stolen the items to return them to the store. The girl threatened her again, but this time she felt the angel's presence and refused to back down. The girl returned the items to the store.

I was told about another situation that involved a woman who discovered her husband was having an affair. She did not know how to handle this, and asked Michael to help her.

During a long conversation with Michael, she discovered that she loved her husband and did not want the affair to end their marriage. She realized that things would never be exactly the same again, but she was prepared to do her part to ensure that the two of them stayed together. She asked Michael to communicate with her husband. Just a few days later, her husband ended the relationship. Apparently, he never knew that Michael had played a part in it. All he knew was that he suddenly felt extremely guilty about what he was doing behind his wife's back. He confessed what he had done to her, and now they are working on improving their relationship.

In this instance, Michael, archangel of truth and integrity, quietly encouraged the husband to be honest and faithful. Michael can help in all sorts of situations that involve truth, honesty, and integrity. All you need to do is ask him to help.

We all face temptation from time to time. Whenever this occurs, it pays to pause and ask Michael for help. In your rituals and during the time you spend in your sacred space ask Michael to help protect you from temptation, and to help you make the right decisions. He will always help you to protect your integrity and honesty in every type of situation.

At any time, if you think what you are planning to do might be unethical or dishonest, pause and ask Michael to clarify the matter for you. Of course, most of the time the answer will be obvious, and you will not need to consult Michael. However, if you are tempted to do it all the same, pause for a few moments and ask Michael. He will provide you with the counsel and advice that you need.

Michael is always prepared to help you whenever you need it. All you need to do is ask. After experiencing the benefits of his wisdom and insight, you will probably want to communicate with Michael every day. We will discuss how and when to do this in the next chapter.

Four

HOW TO CONTACT MICHAEL EVERY DAY

ONCE you start communicating with Michael, you will wonder how you managed to live your life without his aid and protection. However, you must not call on him every time you experience a minor problem or difficulty in your everyday life. Most of the time, you will be able to resolve your problems on your own, or with the help of friends and family. You should call on Michael for help only when the problem is too large or difficult to handle on your own.

All the same, you will benefit enormously from having a brief session with Michael every day. You will find everyday life much easier when you do this. Most people call on divine guidance only in times of difficulty. In practice, it is better to make this a regular part of your life. This is because each contact makes the spiritual connection that much stronger.

This session will help you clarify different situations in your life, gain a sense of where you are going, and give you an opportunity to thank Michael for his care and protection. Every time you do this meditation you will become even closer to Michael. One student told me that she felt she was enfolded in Michael's cloak each time she did this meditation.

The Michael Meditation

If possible, do this meditation at about the same time every day. You might like to meditate while lying in bed at night. Alternatively, you might prefer to lie on the floor in front of your altar. In the summer months, I like meditating outdoors, beside my oracle tree. It makes no difference where or when you perform this meditation.

Ideally, you need to be in a quiet, reflective state of mind. It takes me about thirty minutes to walk to my oracle tree, and I find this time on my own extremely beneficial in preparing myself to contact Michael. In fact, even if I am going to contact Michael indoors, I often go for a walk first, as it restores my soul and helps me forget all the everyday problems of life.

Make yourself as comfortable as possible, and take several deep breaths, holding each breath for a few seconds before exhaling. Allow a wave of relaxation to flow through you each time you exhale.

Mentally scan your body to see if you are totally relaxed, and consciously relax any parts that are still tense. Once you feel totally relaxed, visualize yourself surrounded by pure white light. Allow yourself to bathe in the healing energy of this divine light.

Now it is time to invoke Michael. Say to yourself, silently or out loud: "Archangel Michael, my protector and guide. Thank you for helping me lead a good, honest, worthwhile life. I appreciate all your efforts on my behalf. Please continue to walk with me, and please help, protect, and sustain me every day of my life."

Pause, and wait for a response. Words may appear in your mind, or you might feel a sense of reassurance and comfort. You might even feel yourself enveloped in his wings. People experience Michael in different ways, and the response you receive is likely to vary from time to time. If you are feeling depressed, for instance, you might hear clear words of comfort and support. However, if everything is going well in your life, you might simply experience a sense of knowing that Michael is with you.

Once Michael has responded, thank him again. Now is the time to ask for guidance, protection, or any other form of help. You might, for instance, ask him to walk by your side if you are about to face a difficult or stressful situation. Once you have made your request, offer thanks again.

Sit or lie quietly for a minute or two, then take three deep breaths and open your eyes. You will be able to continue with your day feeling refreshed, revitalized, and with the assurance that Michael is continuing to look after you.

All the people I have spoken to about a daily communication with Michael say that the most important thing for them is the awareness that Michael is always close at hand.

With this certainty in their hearts, they feel that they can withstand any of the difficulties that life might send their way.

A daily communion with Michael reinforces this. The ritual might take only five minutes from start to finish, but will provide life-enhancing hope, comfort, and support. It also demonstrates that you do not need to be a worthy or holy person to enjoy the help of an archangel. Michael is prepared to help you at any time, no matter what you may have done in the past.

Conversation with Michael

When I was seventeen, I read Napoleon Hill's classic book, *Think and Grow Rich,* for the first time. In that book he explained how he had regular imaginary conversations with nine people who had impressed him greatly. He would lie in bed at night, and imagine himself sitting at the head of a table with the people he particularly admired. Over a period of months, these people became more and more real to him, and gave him excellent advice. I experimented with this, and found that it worked extremely well. At the time, my main interest was music and I enjoyed many meetings with famous composers.

One day it occurred to me that if it worked so well with famous people from history, it should work just as well with members of the angelic kingdom. I started having regular conversations with my guardian angel. One evening, I began this ritual with a number of problems on my mind. I asked my guardian angel to invite an archangel to join us, as I felt he would be able to offer more insights into my difficulties. Immediately, Michael appeared, and since then I have enjoyed many long conversations with him.

I have told many people about these conversations over the years, and the usual response is that the communications are not real, and are simply a product of my imagination. This was definitely true at the start. I closed my eyes and imagined myself having a conversation with Michael. However, over a period of time, these conversations became so real and important to me, that I had to determine whether or not they were legitimate. I was sure they were, as I was able to sense Michael's presence each time.

Consequently, I began asking Michael questions about subjects I knew nothing at all about, with the intention of checking them later. Michael found this amusing, and asked why I needed confirmation.

"Surely the fact that we are having a conversation is enough," he told me.

I was forced to agree, and pursued the subject no further. However, the following morning, I found a small white feather beside my bed.

Consequently, although I believe these conversations are real, I cannot prove it. This does not matter, in fact, as I find them a useful and extremely pleasant way of gaining insight into problems and difficulties that would have been hard to resolve in any other way.

There are four steps to enjoying a conversation with Michael:

1. Allow at least thirty minutes in which you will be undisturbed. I talk to Michael while lying in bed at night. However, you can talk with him any time you wish. Make sure that the room is warm, and that you are comfortable.

2. Close your eyes and take several slow, deep breaths. Picture a pleasant scene in your mind. This can be real or imaginary. I change the scenes frequently, but usually choose a pleasant meadow with a stream running through it. In my imagination, I walk across the meadow and lie under a tree by the bank of the stream.

3. Relax in your scene and visualize Michael joining you. You greet each other like the old friends you are, and he sits down beside you. He asks you how you are, and then you open up and tell him everything that is on your mind. Michael listens sympathetically, occasionally nodding his head or smiling. When you've finished, he might ask a question or two before making some suggestions. You can continue conversing until he has provided solutions or guidance to all of your problems.

4. Once you have finished, you take Michael's hand in yours and thank him for his help and friendship. Watch him leave, and then move out of your imaginary scene and return to the present. Take a few deep breaths and open your eyes.

You will find this exercise rewarding and stimulating. It allows you to develop an extremely close relationship with Michael. In effect, it is a serious conversation between two friends. In the course of the conversation, Michael's personality and sense of humor will come through strongly, and you will smile when you recall some of the things he said and did during these sessions. Most importantly, of course, you will find that the help and advice you receive will be invaluable.

There is no reason why you should not talk with Michael every day, if you wish. I might talk to him every day for a week or two, and then not have another conversation for a month. It all depends on what is going on in my life.

There are a number of traditional methods that can also be used to contact angels and archangels. One method that I find helpful is the gentle art of candle burning.

Five

THE MAGICAL POWER
OF CANDLES

C ANDLE burning is an ancient art that has stood the test of time. Candles look attractive, focus the mind, and aid concentration.

Candles are romantic, mood setting, colorful, and comforting. It is no wonder that they are still popular, even when most people nowadays simply flick a switch to enjoy light. Another major benefit of candles is that they tell the angels you are ready to work with them.

A lit candle sends an immediate message to Michael, Raphael, Gabriel, and Uriel. An unlit candle represents the element Earth, but when it is lit it symbolizes all four elements: Fire (Michael), Earth (Uriel), Air (Raphael), and Water (Gabriel). The flame obviously relates to the Fire element, the smoke relates to Air, and the melting wax symbolizes Water. The candle itself represents Earth.

Consequently, the archangels also relate to the four triplicities of astrology:

Aries, Leo, and Sagittarius are *Fire* signs (Michael)

Taurus, Virgo, and Capricorn are *Earth* signs (Uriel)

Gemini, Libra, and Aquarius are *Air* signs (Raphael)

Cancer, Scorpio, and Pisces are *Water* signs (Gabriel)

The four triplicities and the four elements are closely connected to the Cherubim seen in the vision of Ezekiel (Ezekiel 1:4–28). Ezekiel saw four living creatures, each of whom had four faces: the face of a man, a lion, an ox, and an eagle. This can be looked at in this way:

The face of a man relates to Aquarius and Air

The face of a lion relates to Leo and Fire

The face of an ox (bull) relates to Taurus and Earth

The face of an eagle relates to Scorpio and Water

As we already know, the four archangels also look after the four cardinal directions. Combining all of this, and adding the traditional colors for each sign of the zodiac, we get:

Aries—Fire, South, Michael, red, crimson

Taurus—Earth, North, Uriel, green

Gemini—Air, East, Raphael, yellow, brown

Cancer—Water, West, Gabriel, silver, white

Leo—Fire, South, Michael, gold, yellow

Virgo—Earth, North, Uriel, brown

Libra—Air, East, Raphael, blue, green

Scorpio—Water, West, Gabriel, deep red

Sagittarius—Fire, South, Michael, purple

Capricorn—Earth, North, Uriel, black

Aquarius—Air, East, Raphael, blue, gray

Pisces—Water, West, Gabriel, violet, blue

Michael is traditionally related to Leo and the color gold. Consequently, a gold candle can be used to symbolize him. You can burn a gold candle on your altar any time you wish. In fact, you are not limited to your altar, as you can burn gold candles anywhere.

You can also choose a candle that relates to your zodiac sign to symbolize you. If you are, for example, an Aquarian, you would choose a blue or gray candle to represent you. Consequently, you could create a ritual on your altar that involved a gold candle (Michael) and a blue candle (you).

You could also add to this, if you wished, by including a candle that related to your specific request. Here is a list of candle colors, with the attributes they possess:

Red—courage, strength, enthusiasm, love, sex

Orange—honesty, integrity, attraction, adaptability

Yellow—strength, communication, friendship

Green—healing, fertility, truth, luck, happiness

Blue—honesty, sincerity, thoughtfulness, spirituality

Indigo—piety, faith, truth, humanitarianism

Violet—spirituality, power, ambition, healing

White—purity, honesty, innocence, truth

Pink—love, marriage, romance, beauty, hope

Gray—Wisdom, maturity, common sense

Brown—practicality, feet on the ground, steady progress

If your ritual involved protection, for instance, you might choose to use a red or yellow candle. If your ritual involved truth and integrity you would probably choose orange, green, blue, indigo, or white.

There is no limit to the number of candles you can use. However, less is usually more, and a single white candle can be used for any purpose. I frequently use one, two, or three candles in my rituals, but seldom use more. Many years ago, I saw a film called *Carrie*, in which a ridiculous number of candles were used. No extra benefits are gained from using dozens of candles, and they create a potential fire hazard.

Dressing Your Candles

Your candles should be dressed, or anointed, before using them in any ritual. A number of different oils can be purchased for specific purposes. However, there is no need to search out strange and exotic oils. In practice, I have found that the best quality olive oil you can find works extremely well for all purposes.

Start by rubbing oil onto both of your hands, and rub them together. Hold the candle near the middle, and start rubbing oil from the center of the candle up to the wick. Rub in an upwards direction only. Once the top half of the candle has been dressed, oil the bottom half in the same way, rubbing from the center down to the base.

Think of your reason for doing this while dressing your candle. This helps to imprint your purpose into the candle.

Winding the Candle

This is the final stage of preparation. Hold the candle and think about how you intend using it. Wind a length of thin ribbon around the candle, starting at the bottom and finishing at the top. This binds your intention into the candle. Once you have done this to all of the candles you intend using, you can start performing your ritual.

Petitioning Michael Ritual

This is a sample ritual, which you can change as much as you wish to suit your own requirements. Let's assume that you are a Gemini. You have done something you are ashamed of, and want to discuss the matter with Michael.

You might start by dressing and binding three candles: a gold one for Michael, a yellow one for you, and a blue one to represent honesty.

Place these on your altar. The gold candle should be in the center, with the yellow candle placed on the left-hand side and the blue candle on the right. Light the gold candle first, followed by the yellow and then the blue.

Kneel or sit down in front of your altar and gaze at the burning candles. After a minute or two, ask Michael to join you. You might say out loud: "Archangel Michael, please come to my aid. I have done wrong and need your help. Please help me decide what to do."

Continue to stare at the candles, focusing on the flame of the gold candle. Wait expectantly. In a while, something will make you realize that Michael is with you. The candles might flicker, the temperature of the room might alter, or you may simply experience a knowing inside yourself that he is with you.

Once you know that he has arrived, you can speak to him. Tell him exactly what happened. There is no need to use formal or old-fashioned language. Speak to him as if he is an old friend. In the example above, you might say: "Archangel Michael, I have done something very foolish, and I don't know what to do. I was at the water cooler and a group of us started gossiping about Sonia. We were laughing and saying unkind things about her. It wasn't meant to be anything, really. We all said things we shouldn't have. And then someone told Sonia about it. I feel bad, really bad. I know I should apologize, but what if I make everything worse? What if she's angry, or refuses to talk to me? What should I do?"

When you have finished explaining the situation, sit quietly and wait for Michael's reply. You may hear words in your mind, or possibly experience a sudden awareness of what to do. Frequently, you will not receive an immediate reply. In this instance, the reply will come when Michael is ready to respond.

No matter what happens at this stage, end the ritual by thanking Michael for his help and comfort. You might say: "Thank you, Michael. I appreciate you taking the time to listen to me. I know I behaved badly, but I intend making amends, and will try to act in a way that will make you proud of me in the future. Thank you, Michael. Goodbye." Pause for about half a minute, and then put out the candles, snuffing out the candle that symbolizes Michael last.

Naturally, you will have to follow through on the advice that Michael has given you. In this example, he is likely to suggest that you apologize to Sonia. Be assured that the advice that Michael gives you will always be the best course of action for everyone concerned. He will not make life easy for you, but will ensure that you lead a life full of integrity and honor.

This ritual was done with three candles, one for Michael, one for you, and one for the purpose of the ritual. You could also do this ritual with two candles, one for you and one for Michael. You might decide to use just one candle, and that would symbolize Michael. Be guided by what feels right for you at the time.

A Letter to Michael

Another way in which candles can be used to contact Michael involves writing a letter to him. No one will see this letter, so you can write whatever you wish. Make sure that you include sufficient details, and that you clearly explain what you desire from Michael. Once you have finished writing it, seal it in an envelope.

Again, you can use as many, or as few, candles as you wish. Sit in front of your altar and gaze at the candle(s). Hold the letter in your hands, and think of your purpose in writing it. When you feel ready, burn the letter in the candle that symbolizes Michael. Think of your request while it is burning. Once it has totally disappeared, give thanks to Michael for helping you, and put the candles out. The candle that represents Michael should be put out last. Carry on with your life, confident that Michael will attend to the matter on your behalf.

You can also burn a letter if you want to get a message to someone, but do not feel able to speak to him or her yourself. Write the letter to this person, and seal it in an envelope. Address the envelope.

Light a single candle to symbolize Michael. Ask him to deliver the letter to the person's guardian angel for you. If you sense a positive response from Michael, burn the letter, confident that he will deliver the message to the person's guardian angel who will, in turn, deliver the message for you.

There will be times, though, when Michael will not be prepared to accede to this request. In these instances, he is teaching you to be brave. You will either have to post the letter at a post office, or contact the person in some other way.

Naturally, this changes the ritual enormously. When this occurs, ask Michael for the necessary courage and strength to do what he suggests. It might be difficult, but you will be grateful afterward that he forced you to act honorably and ethically.

Candle Burning for Protection

Psychic attack is a fairly rare phenomenon, fortunately, but can occur. Surrounding yourself with a circle of lit candles is an effective antidote, as candles symbolize light, and deter the black magic that is being directed at you.

It is more likely that you will burn candles for other protective purposes. You will need some space, as you will be sitting inside a circle of at least four candles. Choose white candles for this, although you can also include a gold one, for Michael, if desired. If you use a gold candle, it should be placed in the southernmost part of the circle.

Light as many candles as you desire to make up the circle, but ensure that you have three unlit white candles in the center of the circle. Stand inside the circle and face East. In a strong voice ask Raphael for his protection. You might say: "Archangel Raphael, I need your help." Turn to the South and ask Michael for his help and protection. Turn to the West and ask Gabriel for his protection. Turn to the North and ask Uriel for his protection. Visualize these four archangels, with wings outstretched, surrounding your circle of candles, ready to help and protect you.

Turn to the South, so that you are facing Michael. Pick up one of the unlit candles and light it, holding it in front of you at around chest-height. Say: "Michael, Angel of Light, and protector of mankind. Protect me from the darkness, and keep me in the light. This small candle is a symbol of your energy. With your help, I will fear no evil, and will walk in the light always."

Sit down inside the circle facing South, and place the lit candle in a candleholder. Still sitting, light a second candle to symbolically double your protection. Light the third candle to triple it. Place these in candleholders. Hold your hands out in a gesture of supplication, and thank Michael for his help and protection.

Sit inside the circle of candles for as long as you wish. When you feel ready, stand up and bow to Raphael in the East. Thank him for his protection as you do this. Repeat with Michael, Gabriel, and Uriel. Put out all the candles, starting from the East and moving around in a clockwise direction.

Protecting Others

With the help of Michael, you can use the incredible power of candles to send protection to others. Place a white or gold candle on your altar. Light it, and gaze at the flame for a few seconds before sitting down in front of them.

Think of the person or persons you wish to send Michael's protection to. See if you can mentally superimpose their images over the flickering flame of the candle. Call on Michael. You might say: "Archangel Michael, my protector and guide, please come to me." Wait until you sense his presence. "Archangel Michael, thank you for answering my call. I have need of your help. My friend so-and-so is in great need of protection. Would you please help him/her?"

Wait for a response, and then thank him sincerely. Visualize your friend, surrounded by a clear white light of protection. Allow the circle of light to gradually expand until you are both inside it. Thank Michael again. Snuff out the candle, and carry on with your day.

Forgiving Others Ritual

I doubt that anyone has managed to get through life without being hurt by others. Frequently, this hurt comes from the people we love the most. These slights are often unintentional, but people hang on to them and make them worse in their own minds. A knot appears in their stomachs each time they relive each moment of the painful incident. They lie sleepless in bed thinking of the responses they should have made. Long after the person who caused the hurt has forgotten about the incident, the recipient may still be suffering from it, weeks, months, or even years later.

Of course, the sensible thing is to forgive the person who caused the slight and then let go of it, but this is not an easy thing to do. However, it is essential. The emotional suffering will continue until you make up your mind to let it go. Fortunately, Michael can come to your aid and help you achieve this.

You will need a white candle, and some writing implements. When you feel ready to forgive the person who hurt you, place a white candle in the center of your altar. Place the pen and paper on the altar in front of it. Light the candle and sit down in front of your altar. Gaze at the flickering flame and think about the person who has hurt you.

Realize that we all do the very best that we are capable of at any given moment. What the other person did to you was unacceptable. However, it happened. Although you are forgiving him or her, you are not giving permission for the behavior to be repeated in the future. Think about what was actually done to you. This is what needs to be forgiven. You suffered as a result of it, of course, but your feelings were created by you. It is the incident itself that needs to be forgiven.

There is no point in asking why the person acted in the way he or she did. Even if you knew, it would not lessen the pain. Most of the time, the person who hurt you does not know, anyway.

Acknowledge your role in the incident. Had you, deliberately or inadvertently, caused the incident to occur? Did you stay, when it would have been better to walk away? Did you hide your hurt and tell the other person that everything was all right, when it obviously wasn't? If this was not the first time this person had hurt you, why had you not left long ago? There must have been some benefits for you in staying. Accepting any responsibility you have for these helps you cease to be a victim.

Now it is time to write a letter to the person who hurt you. This person will never see the letter, so you can write down anything you wish. Recall some of the good times the two of you enjoyed together, if, in fact, there were any. Write down some of the hurtful things that occurred and express how they made you feel. Tell him or her of your anger, rage, and impotence. Express your forgiveness for all the hurts this person did to you. Write down anything else that seems relevant or important. Tell the person that you have forgiven him or her, and are willing to forget the incident(s). What was done, was done, and it now belongs only to the past. You have let the matter go, and are not going to look back in anger. Add anything else you wish. At the end, write: "I forgive you unconditionally," and sign your name.

Read through the letter a couple of times and make any changes you wish. Once you are certain that the letter is complete, and you have included everything you want to mention, place it in an envelope and write the recipient's name on the front. Place the envelope on the altar in front of the candle.

Ask Michael to give you the help and protection you require as you get ready to burn the envelope. Wait until you feel his presence, and then set fire to the envelope while forgiving the person who hurt you. If possible, express your forgiveness out loud. Imagine the person you are forgiving gaining benefit from your ritual, and ceasing their unacceptable behavior.

Be careful while burning the envelope. You might like to use tongs to hold the envelope while it burns. Alternatively, once it is alight, you might want to place the burning envelope into a container that will contain the flames.

When the letter has completely burned, thank Michael for his assistance and help in every area of your life. Snuff out the white candle and carry on with your life. You will notice a number of immediate changes. Without the burden of bitterness and pain, you will feel happier, lighter, and full of energy.

You may have to repeat this ritual a number of times if the forgiveness relates to a partner or relative. Most of the time, forgiving the incident, and sending that forgiveness out into the universe, is all that is required. However, if the problem relates to long-term abuse, you may need to repeat this ritual regularly to achieve the desired results. In your quiet times with Michael, ask him for his advice as to how often you should repeat this ritual.

Everything we do has an effect, good or bad. Forgiving others is beneficial to you, and can lessen the karmic effects gained by the person who hurt you. Michael can help you deal with your own karma. This is the subject of the next chapter.

Six

KARMA

K ARMA is the law of cause and effect. It means that everything we think or do, good or bad, has an effect later on. A good deed done today will result in something pleasant occurring in the future. Something bad done today will result in a negative experience in the future. What happens to you in the future is caused by your actions in the past. The law is completely impartial.

Complicating this is karma that you brought into this lifetime from previous incarnations. This is why life sometimes seems unfair, as most people have no conscious memories of their previous lifetimes. This also explains how bad things sometimes happen to good, decent people.

Karma is actually a learning process. It is not meant to be "an eye for an eye, a tooth for a tooth" type of process. It assures ultimate, absolute justice for everyone. Once you understand that you are creating all the bad things that occur in your life, you can do something about it. Michael is prepared to help you see the overall pattern, and become aware of what you are doing.

Every day, everything you do, and everything you think, is either creating good or bad karma. Consequently, you may think the situation is hopeless, and you might as well give up right away. However, this solves nothing as, before you were incarnated this time, you chose to be you. If you had not made that decision, you would not be here at this very moment. Obviously, you cannot remember making this choice, as you are now locked in a physical body with a human brain. You are in this incarnation to learn, and to grow in knowledge and wisdom. Asking Michael to help us resolve karmic issues is part of that.

All of the archangels can help you resolve karmic issues. However, Michael has more control over this than the others, and is known as the "Guardian of Karma." Michael can help you clear your karmic debts, by allowing you to see what they are, and what created them. If you recognize the factors involved, you will be able to avoid similar situations in the future. Michael can also provide you with the necessary courage to do the things you need to do to break the cycle.

Imagine waking up to a morning in which you felt totally in control, at peace with yourself and everyone else in the world, and completely free of stress, anxiety, and fear. This may sound like an impossible dream, but once you face your karma and resolve it, that is the life you will be able to enjoy.

Fortunately, Michael is ready and willing to help you achieve it. You can do this with a series of meditations.

Karma Release Meditation

Choose a time when you will not be disturbed. It is not a good idea to do this meditation in bed, or when you are feeling tired, as you are likely to fall asleep, instead of releasing karma. If possible, have a bath or shower and change into something comfortable. Sit back in a recliner-type chair, or maybe lie down on the floor in front of your altar.

If you wish, you can light candles, and play relaxing music. If you burn candles, ensure they are in secure candleholders.

I like to start by facing all four directions in turn and inviting Gabriel, Michael, Raphael, and Uriel to join me. When I feel their presence, I lie down on the floor and commence the meditation. It is not necessary to start this way, but I find it rewarding and satisfying in its own right, and it ensures that I have the archangels with me from the commencement.

Once you lie down, focus on your breathing for a minute or two. Take slow, deep breaths, holding the breath for a few moments before exhaling. Feel your entire body relaxing with each exhalation. Take as much time as you need in this first stage. You need to be totally relaxed to proceed further.

When you feel completely relaxed, visualize yourself surrounded by a powerful ray of healing white light that completely fills the room or area you are within. Allow this white light to gradually expand until it fills the building you are in, and then feel it grow to fill your town, country, and ultimately the entire world. With each exhalation imagine that you are sending healing energy to the whole world.

Now it is time to call on Michael. If you started this meditation by summoning the four archangels, he will already be in the room, and you will be able to sense his presence. If you have not already called on Michael, ask him to join you. Lie peacefully, breathing slowly and steadily, until you become aware that Michael is with you.

Thank Michael for his guidance and protection, and then tell him that you want to resolve some of the karmic factors that have been holding you back, and preventing you from moving forward in this incarnation. Ask him to show you some specific examples, both from this lifetime and any previous incarnations.

Continue to relax comfortably and see what happens. Images from your past may appear in your mind's eye. You may sense certain occurrences. You may feel a tightening in your chest, or an urge to cry.

Try not to do or say anything. Lie quietly and allow everything that Michael is prepared to show you unfold. Be totally nonjudgmental. There is no need to be alarmed if you did something horrendous in a previous lifetime. It was a different personality who did that evil deed, and even though the soul is the same, you are not the person you were in any of your previous lifetimes.

Absorb the information that comes through. When it is over, thank Michael for bringing it to you. Ask him what you can do to release the karmic blocks that are affecting your life. You may receive an immediate answer. Something might appear in your mind to clarify the situation, and by the time you finish the meditation, you will know exactly what steps to take to start releasing any negative karma. It is more likely that the answer will come to you one or two days later. It will probably come when you are doing something completely different, and least expect it.

Once you reach this stage in the meditation, thank Michael again. Become aware of where you are and start to feel the presence of Raphael, Gabriel, and Uriel. Thank them also for their care and support.

Take three deep breaths, exhaling strongly, but in a jerky manner, releasing a small amount of breath each time. As you do this, picture your breath as a healing energy that is going out into the world to help others.

When you feel ready, slowly open your eyes, stretch, and smile. Think about the meditation, and what you experienced, for a few minutes before carrying on with your day.

What happens if Michael does not give you any examples of karma-creating factors? This doesn't mean that you have no karma to repay. No one is perfect, and you can be certain that you, along with everyone else in the world, have accumulated plenty of karma. There could be a number of reasons why Michael does not show these to you. You may not be sufficiently relaxed, for instance. Michael may think you are not taking the subject seriously enough. Michael might feel that the karma you have picked up would be unduly stressful for you to handle at this moment.

Michael's Sword

Many people like to use the symbolism and imagery of Michael's sword when working on releasing karma. It can be helpful to ask Michael to cut the psychic cords that bind you to people, situations, objects, and negativity. You should do this regularly, before situations get out of control. You can also ask Michael to release the karmic factors between groups of people, even entire countries. You may not feel that you can achieve very much on your own, but every bit helps, and if enough people start doing it, enormous changes can be made.

There is a three-step process that I find extremely useful for releasing personal karma.

1. Make yourself comfortable, close your eyes, and take several slow, deep breaths. Gradually relax all the muscles of your body, starting either at your feet and working upward, or from the top of your head and going downward. Once you feel you are totally relaxed, mentally scan your body for any areas that are still tense. Focus on these until they are also completely relaxed.

2. Visualize yourself, as if you were several feet in the air, looking down on your relaxed body. When you can see yourself clearly in your mind's eye, visualize your physical body gradually morphing into a large round ball of twine. There are many strands running off this ball, and going in different directions. These are all attachments to karmic experiences.

Picture yourself inside the ball, and see Michael appear in front of you. He is tall, strong, and dressed in chain mail. He is wielding a large, flaming blue sword in his right hand, and carrying a shield in his left. As you watch, he cuts all the strands of twine until the ball is round and perfect again. Thank him for releasing your karma.

3. The final stage is to take three slow, deep breaths, and then count from one to five. Open your eyes, stretch, and think about what has just happened. Repeat this exercise as often as you wish, until you feel that karma is no longer adversely affecting your life.

Not everyone likes to imagine him- or herself as a large ball of twine. If this is the case with you, relax and, in your mind's eye, see yourself lying on the floor with minute strands of karma going off in all directions. Then visualize Michael standing on your right-hand side, holding his sword up high. Watch him cut all the fine strands of karma close to your body. Notice how much freer and lighter you feel once he has done this.

You are not likely to experience an instantaneous release of karma after performing these exercises. However, they make a start, and you will notice gradual improvements in your life right away.

The next thing you need to do is to work on yourself. You must let go of past hurts, bitterness, regrets, disappointments, and other pain. When your subconscious mind is full of negative thoughts and experiences, it becomes extremely difficult to progress. Eliminating the negative aspects of your past enables you to move forward again. A great deal of karma can be released in this way, also. Most people hang on to these negative experiences, endlessly reliving difficult times in their lives, even though they know it is much healthier and better for them to let those things go and to start moving forward again.

There is an experiment you can do with Michael that will enable you to see the life you will enjoy once you let go of the past. You will find it healing and exciting. Once you release all the baggage that has been holding you back, you will be able to move forward more confidently than ever before. New opportunities will miraculously appear, and every area of your life will improve.

Into the Future Meditation

1. Start by following the Invocation Ritual in chapter 2. When you reach the stage where you ask Michael for help, sit down, close your eyes, and ask him to help you see what your life will be like once you eliminate all the baggage that is holding you back.

2. Focus on your breathing and wait to see what pictures appear in your mind. As everyone is different, it is impossible to say how you will experience these. You may see them clearly, as if they were on a television screen. Alternatively, you might sense them, hear them, or gradually develop an awareness of the future that is rightfully yours.

3. You will find that your mind will drift from scene to scene. Spend as much time as you wish with each of these. When you are ready to proceed to the next one, take a deep breath and exhale slowly. You will automatically find yourself moving to another situation or experience in your future life.

4. When you have experienced enough, thank Michael for giving you the opportunity to see the new direction your life could take, and return to the present, sitting comfortably in your room, surrounded by the four archangels. Become aware of the situation in the room, and when you feel ready, open your eyes.

5. Stand up and complete the Invocation Ritual by giving thanks and performing the banishing pentagram.

6. As soon as possible after this exercise, write down everything you can remember about the experience. Think about what has occurred and the insights that came to you. If you have any doubts that this proposed future is better than the future you would otherwise have had, perform the entire experiment again, but this time ask Michael to show you the future you will have if you keep on the path you are already on. In some ways, it is a good thing to do this anyway. I know a number of people who have been sufficiently motivated by the contrasting futures to totally change their lives.

7. Repeat this exercise several times over the next few weeks to clarify everything in your mind. Write down anything that occurs to you about the experience as soon as possible afterward.

Once you have discovered how different your life will be once you've eliminated the negative karma from the past, you will be motivated to work on it. There are many ways to eliminate this negativity, but I have found three methods particularly useful. If you wish, you can call on Michael to help you in these exercises. However, it is not necessary, unless you want his protection around you while doing them. In that case, work inside a circle and do the invocation ritual before starting to release your karma.

The simplest method is to stand in front of a mirror, look into your eyes, and forgive yourself. Talk out loud. Acknowledge your past mistakes, and tell yourself that from this day on you will strive to be a better person. Speak seriously, and with expression. When you have said everything that you want to say, ask yourself to let go of all the accumulated baggage, so that you can move ahead again. When you have finished, smile at yourself, take three deep breaths, and then carry on with your day.

You will experience an immediate sense of release and relief. Repeat this exercise every day until you are certain that you have succeeded.

A more dramatic way of releasing the past is through dancing. Wear loose-fitting clothes and make sure that you will not be disturbed for at least thirty minutes. Choose music that appeals to you. It is better not to use music with familiar lyrics, as this can prove distracting. You do not want to end up singing the songs, and forgetting the purpose of the exercise.

Dance for several minutes first. Enjoy the physical pleasure of moving your body in time with the music. When you feel ready, continue dancing, but start clapping your hands in time with the music. The final step is to create some words that you can sing along with the music. Something like, "I let go of the past," repeated over and over like a mantra is ideal. Do this for several minutes, while dancing as vigorously as possible. When you feel exhausted, stop, hold out your hands palms upward and say: "I release all of the baggage from my past." Take a deep breath, hold it for a few seconds, and exhale slowly. When you feel ready, continue with your day. As in the previous exercise, do this as often as possible until you feel free of the karma that has been holding you back.

The final example is gentler than the last one, as it is a meditation. Sit or lie down somewhere warm and comfortable, and consciously relax all of the muscles in your body. When you feel totally relaxed, allow your mind to think about what has occurred in your life over the last few months. When you come across anything that involved putting yourself down, or feeling bad, say to yourself, "I release that."

Once you have covered the last few months, start thinking about the previous twelve months. Release anything that you come across that is holding you back. Keep going back year by year as far as possible. As you get closer to your childhood, you will probably need five-year periods of time.

When you get back as far as you can, say, "I release all the karma from my past lives." Allow yourself to gradually return to the present, year by year. Dwell for as long as you wish on any pleasant memories. Release any negative memories you may come across. Once you have reached the present time, take three deep breaths, stretch, and carry on with your day. Do this as frequently as possible until all the baggage has been released.

In the next chapter we will learn how crystals can help us become even closer to Michael.

Seven

CRYSTALS

C RYSTALS, jewels, and gemstones have been considered sacred for almost as long as people have been on this planet. They play a part in the history of all the great religions. The ancient Egyptians, for instance, used crystals for both medicinal and spiritual purposes.

Crystals and gemstones are mentioned many times in the Bible, showing how knowledgeable and skilled ancient people were with their use. The most famous example of this is the breastplate worn by Aaron, the High Priest of Israel (Exodus 28:15–30). In the Book of Revelation, St. John described his vision of a "new Jerusalem" (Revelation 21:9–21). In verses 19 and 20, he wrote: "And the foundations of the wall of the city were garnished with all manner of precious stones. The first foundation was jasper; the second, sapphire; the third, chalcedony; the fourth, emerald.

The fifth, sardonyx; the sixth, sardius; the seventh, chryso-lite; the eighth, beryl; the ninth, topaz; the tenth, chryso-prasus; the eleventh, jacinth; the twelfth, amethyst."

For me, the interesting part of St. John's words is that each gemstone represented a certain aspect of life. What these were is not known, but many people later associated differ-ent qualities with them. In 786 C.E., Rabanus Maurus, Arch-bishop of Mainz, associated each gemstone to one of the twelve apostles.[1] In time, the gemstones became associated with different months of the year. In fact, even in many churches today, the vessel that holds the sacred host symbol-izing Jesus is often surrounded by twelve gemstones.

The Council of Laodicea discouraged the use of gem-stones. However, the Pope still presents new cardinals with a red hat and a sapphire ring. The Pope wears an amethyst.

Interestingly, there is an old Jewish legend that tells how Michael's tears turned into precious stones. God sent Michael to tell Abraham that his life was at an end. Abra-ham met a stranger, and invited him to his home. He had no idea that the stranger was an angel, let alone Archangel Michael. While the servants were preparing a meal, Abra-ham asked Isaac, his son, to bring a bowl of water so that he could wash the feet of the stranger. Abraham looked in the bowl, and said, "I fear this is the last time I will wash the feet of a guest." When he heard this, Isaac began to cry. Abraham also started to weep, and Michael, seeing them cry, began weeping also. His tears fell into the bowl and were transformed into precious jewels.[2]

In the Islamic tradition, Michael delivers his weekly ser-mons from a pulpit made of green emerald in the House of

God in the fourth heaven. This House is full of precious gemstones. There is a prayer niche made of pearls, and a dividing curtain made of numerous gems. The House contains three doors. One is made of topaz, another of green beryl, and the third is made of red gold. The minaret is made entirely of diamonds.[3]

Crystals have always enjoyed a close association with the angelic realms. Consequently, a few attractive crystals on your altar will encourage angels to visit you. They also make it easier for you to communicate with them to receive help and guidance.

Pope Gregory ascribed the carbuncle (a garnet cut in a convex, rounded shape without facets) to the archangels.[4] Gradually, different gemstones were ascribed to all the better-known angels:

Gemstone	Angel(s)
Agate	Raphael, Bariel
Alexandrite	Geburathiel
Amethyst	Uriel, Zadkiel, Adnachiel
Angelite	Uriel
Aquamarine	Michael, Asariel, Humiel
Aventurine	Raphael
Carnelian	Camael
Charoite	Zadkiel
Chrysoprase	Raphael
Citrine	Jophiel, Caneloas

Gemstone	*Angel(s)*
Diamond	Camael, Israfel, Hamatiel
Emerald	Raphael, Anael, Muriel
Garnet	Amriel
Jasper	Barchiel
Kunzite	Chamuel, Atar
Lapis lazuli	Michael, Zadkiel
Malachite	Nadiel
Moonstone	Gabriel, Ofaniel
Obsidian	Cassiel
Onyx	Cassiel, Gabriel
Opal	Anael, Nibra Ha-Rishon
Orthoclase	Metatron
Pearl	Gabriel, Nelle
Peridot	Alair
Ruby	Camael, Malchadiel
Sapphire	Raphael, Ashmodei, Verchiel
Sardonyx	Derdekea
Selenite	Gabriel
Spinel	Raziel
Tanzanite	Gabriel
Tiger's eye	Michael
Topaz	Azrael, Ashmodel, Matthew
Tourmaline	Haniel, Tadhiel
Turquoise	Michael, Zadkiel, Verchiel
Zircon	Tsuriel

Blue and gold crystals are the most effective crystals to use when contacting Michael. Tiger's eye, aquamarine, turquoise, and lapis lazuli are good examples. Remember that you can also use a quartz crystal when communicating with the angelic realms.

Most of the time, your crystals will seem to choose you. If you browse in a crystal store, you are likely to find that some of the gemstones will mysteriously call out to you, and you will find yourself attracted to them for some, apparently, unknown reason. I always buy stones that communicate with me in this way. This means that I may set out to buy a couple of rose quartz crystals, but return home with an emerald and a citrine.

Even when this does not occur, use your intuition to help you choose the right gemstones. Hold them in your hands, close your eyes for a few seconds, and see what response you receive. Some crystals appear happy, while others seem thoughtful and quiet. Some crystals seem warm, while others feel cold. Some tingle and pulsate. They are all different. Take your time and ensure that you choose the crystals that are meant for you.

Cleansing Your Crystal

You must cleanse your crystal before using it. This removes any negative energies it may have picked up before it came into your possession. If you have not used the crystal before, leave it overnight in a glass containing sea or salt water. The water will absorb the negative energy from the crystal, while the salt will break down the negativity and eliminate it.

After the initial cleansing, you can cleanse your crystal any time you wish by washing it in running water. An alternative is to use lukewarm water and a small amount of good-quality soap. If you are in a hurry, you can cleanse your crystal by breathing on it. Hold it between your first finger and thumb of your left hand while taking three deep breaths. Visualize yourself inhaling pure white light. After the third breath, blow the healing white light onto the crystal. Move the crystal around to ensure that you cover all of it with your breath. You can also cleanse your crystal according to your astrological element:

If you belong to the element of *Fire* (Aries, Leo, Sagittarius), pass your crystal through the flame of a lit candle. Alternatively, create a circle of candles and rest your crystal in the center. Burn the candles for at least three hours.

If you belong to the element of *Earth* (Taurus, Virgo, Capricorn), bury your crystal in earth for twenty-four hours. To complete the process, wash the crystal in purified water.

If you belong to the element of *Air* (Gemini, Libra, Aquarius), hold your crystal in the smoke from a burning candle. An even better method is to hold it in the smoke from a smudge stick.

If you belong to the element of *Water* (Cancer, Scorpio, Pisces), hold your crystal under running water. Tap water will work, but if possible, find a running stream or waterfall. Alternatively, wash it in the sea. If you do this, you must rinse it in pure water afterward to eliminate any residue of salt.

If your crystal becomes exposed to negative energies, the best remedy is to bury it in earth for a few days. This will restore it to balance.

Charging Your Crystal

Once your crystal has been cleansed, you will need to charge it to fill it with natural energy. There are two types of energy, male and female. The type of energy you require is determined by the purpose you intend dedicating the crystal to. If you are charging it for protection, you would choose male energy. However, if your purpose is to improve your intuition, you would choose female energy. If you desire male energy, lie your crystal in sunlight for a few hours. For female energy, place it in the light of the moon.

Leaving your crystal out in the rain, or keeping it outside overnight to receive dew, are effective ways of charging your crystal. If you need plenty of energy, you should put your crystal outside in a thunderstorm. This will provide a virtually unlimited supply of power. If you use your altar regularly, you can charge your crystals by placing them on top of the altar.

Dedicating Your Crystal

Once your crystal has been cleansed and charged, you can dedicate it to whatever purpose you desire. Naturally, for the purposes of this book, you will dedicate it to Michael.

Light two candles, one gold and one blue, and place these on your altar. Sit down in front of your altar, with the crystal resting on your right palm. Rest the back of your right hand on the palm of your left hand.

Take three deep breaths, exhaling slowly, and then invite Michael to join you. When you feel his presence, raise both hands to about chest height, and say: "I dedicate this crystal to you, Michael, to create a closer bond with you, and to strengthen my ability to receive your guidance. Thank you."

Place the crystal on your altar, and gaze at it for several seconds. Thank Michael for joining you. When you feel ready, snuff out the candles, but leave the crystal on the altar for at least twenty-four hours.

Now that the crystal has been dedicated to Michael, you can gain an instant connection with him whenever you wish by holding the crystal. You can also carry the crystal around with you, if you wish. However, make sure that it is wrapped in a silk cloth, or is placed in a small bag, to prevent it being affected by any negativity.

Keep this crystal cleansed, and re-dedicate it if you feel that it is losing its power. This is unlikely to occur, but can happen.

Crystal Prayer

I like to perform this ritual out of doors, in the summer months. However, it can be done anywhere, at any time. Lie on your back, and place a quartz crystal over your heart. Take several deep breaths and close your eyes.

Start talking to Michael, out loud or mentally. You can say whatever you wish. You might pray, ask questions, ask for advice, or thank him for his love and protection. You will find that the crystal on your heart acts as a "psychic amplifier," making it easier for you to receive Michael's response.

Soul Healing Meditation

Choose two crystals that appeal to you. Allow your intuition to direct you to the two crystals that will be most beneficial to you when performing this meditation.

Sit down in a comfortable chair, with a crystal held loosely in each hand. Take several deep breaths and exhale slowly. Close your eyes and allow a wave of relaxation to go right through your body. Think of all the blessings in your life, and give thanks to the universe for enabling you to receive and enjoy them. Deliberately discard any negative thoughts that may come to your mind. Focus on the positive, and you will realize how rich your life is in so many ways.

Focus on the crystals and notice any sensations you receive from them. You might experience a thought, sensation, or emotion. They might feel warm and comforting. They might tingle slightly. Do not evaluate these responses. Simply accept them, and realize that you can analyze the experience afterward, if you wish.

Ask Michael to join you, and thank him for all his aid, love, support, and comfort. Thank him for helping your physical, mental, emotional, and spiritual beings.

Allow him to touch your soul. Again, you can experience this in many different ways. It may feel as if a sudden burst of electricity has passed through you. You may feel a glowing sensation. (This can be a physical experience also, as I have seen a number of students with flushed faces after performing this meditation.) You may feel a sense that you can achieve anything you set your mind on. You may feel as if all your cares and worries have been taken away.

Stay in this state for as long as you can. Enjoy the feeling of total peace and tranquillity, and realize how much good it is doing for your soul, and every other part of your being.

When you feel the time is right, take a deep breath, hold it for a moment, and exhale slowly. Thank Michael again, squeeze the crystals, and open your eyes.

Take a minute or two to return to the everyday world. You will be full of energy, and will feel restored and revitalized in mind, body, and spirit.

There is always a degree of time distortion with this meditation. Sometimes the entire ritual takes me about five minutes, but I will feel as if it took half an hour. At other times, the same ritual will take thirty or forty minutes, but I will feel as if it was only a few minutes long. I have no idea why this occurs. However, I have learned to allow sufficient time to perform this meditation.

Crystals work well with the chakras, and are frequently used for chakra balancing. We will look at this, and also discuss how the chakras relate to the angelic kingdom, in the next chapter.

Eight

CHAKRAS

THE chakras are wheel-like energy centers located in the aura. They help the transformation and distribution of pranic energies throughout the auric field. They connect the physical and subtle bodies, which is why our emotions are able to affect our physical bodies. They are usually seen as whirling circles of energy. Not surprisingly, *chakra* is a Sanskrit word that means "wheel" or "disk."

The seven main chakras are located along the spine at the following positions:

1. Root Chakra—Base of the Spine
It is concerned with survival, strength, and forgiveness. *Color:* Red. *Archangel:* Sandalphon. *Crystals:* Red garnet, jasper, ruby.

2. Sacral Chakra—The Sex Organs

It is concerned with emotions, sensuality, and sexuality. *Color:* Orange. *Archangel:* Chamuel. *Crystals:* Amber, carnelian, orange calcite, topaz.

3. Solar Chakra—One Inch Below the Navel

It is concerned with self-esteem and willpower. *Color:* Yellow. *Archangel:* Uriel. *Crystals:* Citrine, tiger's eye, yellow jasper.

4. Heart Chakra—Center of the Chest

It is concerned with love, compassion, and acceptance. *Color:* Green. *Archangel:* Raphael. *Crystals:* Emerald, jade, kunzite, aventurine.

5. Throat Chakra—The Throat

Concerning communication, the truth, and creativity. *Color:* Blue. *Archangel:* Michael. *Crystals:* Aquamarine, chrysocolla, lapis lazuli, turquoise.

6. Brow Chakra—Between the Eyebrows ("Third eye")

It is concerned with wisdom, discernment, intuition, and imagination. *Color:* Indigo. *Archangel:* Gabriel. *Crystals:* Blue calcite, lapis lazuli, turquoise.

7. Crown Chakra—The Crown of the Head

Concerned with illumination, understanding, and knowledge. *Color:* Violet. *Archangel:* Zadkiel. *Crystals:* Amethyst, selenite, charoite.

When a chakra is blocked or closed, the person is unable to make full use of the energy available for that particular part of his or her life. If, for example, the throat chakra is blocked, the person will be timid, shy and find it hard to express him- or herself. The other extreme can also occur. When this chakra is wide open, the person will be so busy talking that he or she will not be able to listen to anything anyone else says. This is done at the expense of the other chakras, which will be correspondingly deficient. Both of these extremes cause problems that will not be relieved until the throat chakra is brought back into balance.

The throat chakra is concerned with creativity, another form of communication. When the throat chakra is blocked, or alternatively, wide open, the creative potential is lessened and dissipated.

I have used the throat chakra as an example, because this is the chakra ruled by Archangel Michael. Each chakra is just as important as any other. Any blocked chakra impacts on the effectiveness of all the others.

Chakra Sensing

You will need a partner for this exercise. Your partner should wear loose-fitting, comfortable clothes, and can lie either on his or her front or back, as the chakras can be sensed from both sides of the spine.

Start by performing the protection ritual, and then rub your hands briskly together. Kneel down beside your partner and hold your hands a few inches above his or her body, at the base of the spine. See if you can feel the energy of the chakra in the palms of your hands. Move your hands closer to the spine, and further away, until you find the position that allows you to sense the chakra best.

Once you have sensed the root chakra, move your hands up to the sacral chakra, which is halfway between the root chakra and the navel. Again, experiment with your hand positions until you can sense the chakra. Continue doing this until you have identified all seven chakras.

Once you have done this successfully, change places to allow your partner to locate your chakras.

Your chakras extend from your body like funnels or cones. With practice, you will find that you can feel them when your hands are several inches away from the body.

Chakra Balancing Meditation

As you know, an archangel looks after each chakra. This meditation allows you to use angelic energy to balance and restore your chakras. If you are aware that a particular chakra is out of balance, place a crystal that relates to it on your body, over the area of the chakra.

If you feel like it, use incense or essential oils. You may wish to light a candle, and play some gentle music. Make whatever preparations you feel necessary to ensure a successful meditation.

Wear loose-fitting clothes and ensure that the room is reasonably warm. The best place to perform this ritual is in front of your altar, but anywhere will do, as long as you feel safe and secure, and are not likely to be interrupted.

Lie on your back, with your hands by your sides, and take several slow, deep breaths. Ask Michael to protect you while doing this meditation. Visualize yourself surrounded by a pure white protective light.

When you feel ready, focus on your root chakra. Imagine that part of your body surrounded by a beautiful red glow. If you wish, place your hands over this area. Ask Michael to introduce you to Archangel Sandalphon. Ask him to cleanse, restore, and balance your root chakra. As Sandalphon fulfills this task, enjoy the sensations of security as you become well-grounded once again.

Once Sandalphon has finished, allow yourself to focus on your sacral chakra. Visualize this area suffused in a beautiful orange glow. Again, rest your hands on this area, if you wish. Ask Michael to introduce you to Archangel Chamuel, the angel of unconditional love. Relax and allow Chamuel to balance and revitalize your sacral chakra.

Allow Chamuel as much time as necessary before focusing on your solar chakra. Imagine this area surrounded by a magnificent yellow ray. Place your hands on your solar plexus, if desired. Ask Michael to introduce you to Uriel, archangel of peace. Allow Uriel to balance this chakra, eliminating hurts and fears, and replacing them with peace and harmony.

When Uriel has finished, allow your attention to move up to your heart chakra, which is surrounded by a beautiful, peaceful green. Again, place your hands on this area, if desired. Ask Michael to introduce you to Raphael, archangel of healing and wholeness. Ask Raphael to balance and heal your heart chakra. I have found that many people find balancing this chakra to be highly emotional. Do not worry if this occurs. Allow all the necessary emotion to release itself before moving on to the next chakra.

Focus on your throat and imagine it surrounded by the most beautiful clear blue ray of light. Place your hands on your throat if you feel it will help you visualize it better. This is the chakra that Michael looks after. Relax and allow him to balance and restore this chakra for you. Once he has done this, thank him for his help.

When you feel ready, allow your attention to move to your brow chakra. Visualize this area surrounded by a pure, deep indigo color. Gently rest your hands on this area, if you wish. Ask Michael to introduce you to Gabriel, archangel of the soul. Feel your intuition blossom as Gabriel balances your third-eye chakra.

There is one chakra left. When you feel ready, focus on the crown chakra at the top of your head. Rest your hands on this area if you wish. Imagine the top of your head completely surrounded by an intense violet glow. Ask Michael to introduce you to Zadkiel, archangel of forgiveness. Allow a feeling of peace and tranquillity to spread throughout your entire body as Zadkiel restores and balances your crown chakra.

Once he has done this, thank each archangel individually. Imagine yourself surrounded by red energy as you thank the Archangel Sandalphon. Visualize yourself surrounded by orange light as you thank Chamuel. Go right through the rainbow, imagining yourself being bathed by each color as you thank the different archangels.

Allow yourself to relax and relive the experience in your mind's eye. When you feel ready, take three deep breaths, open your eyes, and get up. You will feel revitalized in your body, mind, and soul after this meditation. Your chakras will be balanced and you will feel positive, enthusiastic, and full of energy. Matters that seemed important before, will now seem trivial and of no account. You will feel ready to achieve anything.

Write down any insights that occurred to you during the process as soon as possible afterward.

Repeat this meditation as often as possible. Once a week would be perfect, but do it more often if you are experiencing problems, such as stress or emotional turmoil, in your life.

When You're Feeling Blue

It is highly appropriate that Michael's color is blue, as it can be used in many ways. Looking at the blue in nature can strengthen the bond between you and Michael. It can also be used for healing. Indigo provides healing energy from the earth. Indigo blue is also calming, relaxing, and peaceful. It also provides wisdom. Cobalt blue is cauterizing in nature, and allows you to eliminate past hurts. It also provides protection. Whenever you feel the need for increased protection, visualize yourself inside a large bubble of cobalt blue. Sky blue provides healing energy from the air. It also reminds you that the sky is the limit. No matter what happened to you yesterday, today is a brand new day, and the blue sky allows you to feel Michael's love and protection, and to realize that you can make today a magnificent success.

Here's an interesting exercise that uses the blue energy from your throat chakra.

1. Lie down on your back, arms and legs apart. Close your eyes, take several slow, deep breaths, and allow yourself to relax and focus inward.

2. Visualize yourself inside a large bubble of clear, white protective light. Once you feel you are safely cocooned inside this bubble, imagine a vertical column inside your body that extends downward, from the top of your head to the base of your spine. It passes through each of the chakras.

3. Visualize Michael standing beside you. He is gazing down at you with love and compassion. He is there to restore your body, mind, and soul. In your mind's eye, picture him kneeling beside you and gently touching the top of your head. See a radiant cobalt-blue energy entering your body through the top of your head and gradually filtering down the vertical column, filling each chakra with healing energy as it goes. Finally, the blue energy reaches your root chakra and then slowly spreads out from each chakra, gradually infusing every cell in your body with Michael's restorative energy.

4. Finally, your physical body is full of Michael's energy, but more blue energy continues to enter your body from the top of your head. It flows down to your

throat chakra and then spreads out into the bubble of clear, white light that surrounds you. Only when this bubble is full of blue energy does Michael take his hand away from your head.

5. Speak to Michael, thanking him for filling you with this restorative energy, and for providing protection and love. Ask him to help you fulfill your potential and become the very best that you possibly can. Talk to Michael for as long as you wish.

6. Say goodbye and watch Michael leave. Enjoy the feelings of safety, security, and energy for as long as you wish. When you feel ready, count slowly from one to five, open your eyes, stretch, and stay lying down for at least thirty seconds before getting up.

You will find this exercise highly beneficial. It provides energy and protection, but also helps you to realize that you are capable of achieving anything you set your mind upon. Consequently, you should perform this chakra exercise frequently.

Michael's Blue Cloak

Whenever you need protection for yourself, or for others, call on Michael and ask him to surround the person requiring protection with his blue cloak of protection. Visualize the person you want to protect completely covered, from head to foot, inside a beautiful cobalt-blue cloak.

If you are doing this for yourself, visualize yourself covered in the cloak of protection. Then imagine blue energy coming from your throat chakra and spreading rapidly throughout your body, until you are completely surrounded by Michael's protective energy, both inside and out. When the need for protection is over, thank Michael for providing the protection, and then mentally take the cloak off.

I like the idea of a cloak of protection. Many of my students prefer to surround themselves with a bubble or circle of protection. This is fine, too, as both methods work equally as well. Use whichever you prefer.

Nine

DREAMING WITH MICHAEL

M OST people spend about a third of their lives sleeping. Although this may seem a huge waste of time, sleep is essential to your health and well-being. This period of rest gives your body time to restore itself. If you fail to get enough sleep at night, you will feel drowsy the next day, and will not be able to perform at your best. People vary in the amount of sleep they require. Some people manage perfectly well on four or five hours of sleep a night, while others need up to nine. Most people need seven or eight hours of sleep a night.

However, even when you are asleep, your body and mind are still active. For instance, you will have four or five periods of REM (rapid eye movement) sleep each night. This is when your important dreams occur. At one time it was thought that we did not dream during the non-REM periods. However, it now appears that we dream routine, unimportant dreams in this non-REM state. All mammals experience REM and non-REM states in their sleep, showing that this is a normal and essential part of life.

People have always been fascinated with dreams. The ancient Egyptians studied them six thousand years ago, and recorded their findings. The Greeks were just as interested, and Zeus, father of the gods, had a son called Morpheus, god of dreams. Many of the Greek shrines were places where people went to have their dreams interpreted. The ancient Chinese were also interested in dream interpretation, as were most other early civilizations.

The first book on dream interpretation dates back to the fourth century C.E. This was *Oneirocriticia,* by Artemidorus.[1] Ancient religious texts contain many references to dreams and their significance. Examples include the Bible, the Bhagavad-Gita, the I Ching, the Koran, the Book of the Dead, and the Torah.

At one time dreams were an important part of Christianity. Numerous dreams are mentioned in the Bible, and it appears that God and his angels regularly communicated with people in their dreams. The angel of God, for instance, spoke to Jacob in a dream (Genesis 31:11), and God, himself, came to Solomon in a dream (I Kings 3:5). The most famous example of this is when the angel of the Lord appeared to Joseph in a dream. The angel told him: "Joseph, thou son of David, fear not to take unto thee Mary thy wife; for that which is conceived in her is of the Holy Ghost" (Matthew 1:20). Peter's dream at Joppa (Acts 11:5–10) was largely responsible for the new church's change in attitude about dietary laws.

Back then, as today, many people refused to listen. In the Book of Job (33:14–16) we read: "For God speaketh once, yea twice, yet man perceiveth it not. In a dream, in a vision of the night, when deep sleep falleth upon men, in slumberings upon the bed; then he openeth the ears of men, and sealeth their instruction."

Many of the early Christians studied their dreams to help them understand how God was working in their lives. Consequently, dreams were considered highly important for at least five centuries after the birth of Christ. Saint John Chrysostom (c. 347–407), one of the early church fathers, claimed that dreams were enough for God to send to those who believed in him, because they had no need for visions or more startling forms of divine revelation.[2] His writing must have comforted many, as he also mentioned that we are not morally responsible for anything that occurs in our dreams, as they are symbolic, rather than actual. Origen (c. 185– 254) believed that God spoke in dreams to benefit not only the dreamer, but also the other people the dreamer spoke to about it.[3]

Synesius of Cyrene believed that dreams provided hope. "When our heart spontaneously presents hope to us, as happens in our sleeping state, then we have in the promise of our dreams a pledge from divinity."[4]

If this was the Christian point of view for five hundred years, why did it suddenly change? The researches of Morton Kelsey and John Sanford may well provide the answer.

They found that when St. Jerome (c. 342–420) translated the Bible into Latin, he deliberately mistranslated a Hebrew word several times so that dream work became a prohibition.[5] St. Jerome's translation became known as the Vulgate Bible and had a huge effect on the development of the Christian church.

St. Gregory (c. 540–604), known as Saint Gregory the Great, was Pope for the last fourteen years of his life. He wrote extensively and created the principles and dogma that the Catholic Church has used ever since. In one of his writings he affirmed the value of dreams, but later wrote on the subject again, warning people about putting faith in their dreams.

Consequently, dreams, which had been so important in the early church, were gradually forgotten until the twentieth century when psychoanalysts began taking an interest in them. Sigmund Freud (1856–1939), for instance, based his analyses largely on his interpretations of his clients' dreams.

Carl Jung (1875–1961) considered dreams to consist of both psychological and spiritual energy. He developed dream working methods that are closely connected to those used in the first centuries of the Christian church. For instance, he believed that the best person to interpret a dream was always the dreamer. This is in line with the thinking of the early church.

Today, Biblical scholars are again looking seriously at dreams as a way of communicating with the divine. After all, God and his angels spoke directly to people in the past in their dreams. There is no reason why this form of communication cannot be used today.

How to Remember Your Dreams

Everyone dreams. In fact, if you did not dream you would become mentally unwell. Many people claim they do not dream, as they fail to remember them. However, it is possible for everybody to learn how to remember their dreams, and gain all the benefits that dream recall offers.

The most useful method I have found is to keep a dream diary beside the bed. As soon as I wake up, even in the middle of the night, I make notes about any dreams I can remember. As I do this, more memories come back to me, and I write these down as well. Everyone I know who has experimented with a dream diary has found it helpful.

I like to jot down my thoughts with pen on paper. You may prefer to record them on a cassette recorder, and then transcribe them to your dream diary later. If you do this, make sure that you transcribe your messages word for word, as some of the meaning may be lost if you try to rearrange your words to make the message read better. Your dream diary is, or should be, private to you, and you need to be totally honest with everything you record in it.

Another method is to tell yourself before falling asleep that you will dream, and will remember the dream in the morning. I usually tell myself that I will dream about a particular subject, and will remember it.

Some people find it helpful to tell other people about their dreams. While they are retelling it, forgotten details come back to them. Unfortunately, most dreams are boring to other people, so you need to choose the people you tell them to carefully.

Sometimes you will wake up, having just had a dream. You know you have been dreaming, but cannot remember it. A useful method of recapturing it is to lie quietly, without changing position, and see what comes to your mind.

Generally, the first thought that comes to your mind after waking up will be connected with a dream. If you think about this thought, you will often recall the final part of the dream, which will then allow you remember it all.

Some people find it helpful to sit up or stand up as soon as they open their eyes. The rationale behind this is that it forces them to wake up completely. They then recall their dream, and write it down.

I find that the opposite works better for me. I have more success at remembering my dreams when I lie quietly in bed with my eyes closed. I go through as much of the dream as possible, to make it clear in my mind. Once I am sure that I have remembered all the relevant details, I open my eyes and write in my dream diary.

Experiment, and see which methods work best for you. Do not worry when you fail to remember anything. You have several dreams every night, so simply try again the next night, and the night after. With practice, you will find yourself remembering your dreams almost every night, and your dream diary will become more and more valuable to you as time goes on.

There are a number of methods of contacting Michael in your dreams.

Dream Request

The simplest method is to make a request to Michael before falling asleep. You might like to write down your question or request, insert it into an envelope addressed to Michael, and put it under your pillow. An acquaintance of mine writes her letters to Michael in the form of a short poem. As well as placing this under her pillow, she also silently says the poem to herself over and over again while she is falling asleep. She claims that her poetical requests are always answered. Naturally, you do not have to write a poem. Write a letter to Michael as if you were writing to a close friend.

Even if you do not write your request down on paper, it is a good idea to think about what you want as you drift off to sleep. This will place it in your subconscious mind.

When you wake up in the morning, the answer to your question will probably be in your mind. If you keep a dream diary by your bed, you will be able to write down anything that occurs to you as soon as you wake up. As you know, dreams quickly fade and disappear from your memory, especially if you have to leap out of bed and get ready for a busy day.

One of my students had an interesting experience while working with this. The company Lydia worked for was being sold and she was worried that she might have to find a new position. She wrote a letter to Michael, telling him about all her concerns, and slept on it. The first morning she received no reply. However, on the next morning Lydia recalled a dream in which she was working with one of her colleagues in a new laboratory.

Lydia was excited and concerned about this. She knew the person she was working with in her dream, but had spoken to her only occasionally, as they worked in different departments. It seemed strange that in her dream they were working together.

After thinking about it all morning, Lydia decided she had nothing to lose, and went to see the person she had been working with in her dream. As soon as Lydia started talking about her dream, the lady she had gone to see put a finger to her lips and closed the door. It turned out that she was well on the way to setting up her own corporation and was looking for good staff. She offered Lydia a position there and then.

Lydia credits Michael with finding her new position.

"I would never, in a million years, have gone and spoken to Carol if she hadn't appeared in my dream. I hardly knew her. Why did she appear in my dream at the very time I was asking Michael for help? The answer is obvious, at least to me. I called on Michael for help, and he gave me the answer in my dream."

Lydia did not ask for a reply in the form of a dream. However, frequently the answer to a request of this sort will come in the form of a relevant dream. At other times, the answer will appear in your mind, either when you first wake up, or later on in the day when you are working on something totally unrelated to the problem.

Prophetic Dreams

There are many famous examples of prophetic dreams. Julius Caesar's wife Calpurnia dreamt that her husband should beware the Ides of March. Unfortunately, although he made good use of his own dreams, Caesar ignored this one, and paid the ultimate price. Abraham Lincoln dreamt of his own funeral shortly before his assassination. Charles Dickens experienced a more typical example of a prophetic dream. He dreamt of a woman, wearing a red shawl, called Miss Napier. He wondered about this when he woke up in the morning, as he knew no one of that name. The following evening, Charles Dickens was introduced to a woman wearing a red shawl, called Miss Napier.[6]

As you work with your dream diary, you will discover that many of your dreams are prophetic. Shortly after I began keeping a dream diary, I dreamt that I was having a cup of coffee with an old school friend. I had not seen my friend for more than ten years, so was surprised when we bumped into each other a couple of weeks later. We went to a coffee lounge to catch up on what we had been doing. If I had not written my dream down in my diary, I may not have been aware of how prophetic my dream had been. Prophetic dreams can be on a small scale, as mine was, or of great importance. The dreams of Calpurnia and Abraham Lincoln could not have been more important.

Michael can help you dream prophetic dreams that will provide you with insight into the future. When you go to bed at night, ask Michael to give you a dream that will show you exactly what life will be like in the future if you take a certain course of action.

Write down everything you can remember as soon as you wake up in the morning. Sometimes you will write down a great deal, but at other times, it will be hard to remember anything of importance. Make your request several days in a row. After a week, your dreams should have given you a good indication of how matters will turn out. With this information, you can decide whether or not to make the move you were considering.

A young friend of mine had decided to take a year off college to travel and, as he put it, "experience life." As he had only one year to go to complete his degree, I suggested he ask Michael for a prophetic dream.

Thomas could not remember his dreams on the first three nights, but on the fourth night he experienced a dream that was so disturbing, he changed his mind. He went back to college for the final year and completed his degree. It was several months before he told me what he had dreamt.

"It was scary," he told me. "In my dream, I saw myself travelling the world and having a great time. But when I came back home, I didn't go back to college. I saw myself working long hours in a furniture store, angry at not finishing my degree, and blaming everyone else for what I'd done."

Thomas is now a successful attorney, and he thanks Michael for showing him how important it was to finish his degree, and then start "experiencing life."

Lucid Dreaming

Lucid dreaming occurs when you are consciously aware that you are dreaming. You can then participate in the dream and lead it wherever you wish. Most people experience this spontaneously every now and again. However, it is a skill that anyone can develop. The term "lucid dreaming" was coined by Frederik van Eeden, a Dutch physician and researcher, who had his first lucid dream in 1897.[7] He wrote a lengthy article on the subject that was published in the *Proceedings of the Society for Psychical Research* in 1913. Unfortunately, he was ahead of his time, and it was many decades before scientists began examining this phenomenon.

Although it appears that almost everyone can learn to lucid dream, people who meditate and frequently remember their dreams find it easier to dream lucidly than people who pay no attention to their dreams.[8]

The first stage of lucid dreaming is to have a dream, and realize in the middle of it that you are dreaming. Most people wake up when they reach this state. However, with practice you can remain in the dream and see where it takes you. Alternatively, you can direct the dream in any direction you wish. You may want to stay with the theme of the dream you are having, but make it more positive or pleasant. This is especially the case with sexual dreams. You might want to change the location and events of the dream entirely. You can travel backward and forward through time, visit people who have been dead for many years and have conversations with them, visit places you have always wanted to see, on this planet or elsewhere, and anything else you may wish to do. Naturally, you can also use your lucid dreams to spend time with Michael.

Of course, you will probably not want to wait until you happen to experience a lucid dream. Fortunately, there are a number of things you can do to encourage lucid dreaming.

Read as much as you can about the subject. This seems to encourage lucid dreams to occur. If you keep a dream diary, you might find it helpful to read about your past dreams, as you may have accidentally had a number of lucid dreams without realizing it. Dreams of flying, for instance, are sometimes lucid dreams.

You can tell yourself before you fall asleep that you will experience a lucid dream during the night, and will use it to achieve a certain goal. This method works well for some people, but I find that it works for me only some of the time.

Another method that many people find helpful is to tell themselves that when they happen to see their hands in a dream they will immediately start lucid dreaming. Again, I find this method works for me only some of the time.

The most reliable method I have found is to set my alarm clock so that it wakes me up about four hours after I have gone to sleep. When it rings, I turn it off and if I have been dreaming, return to my dream.

The first few times you try this, you will probably find that your awareness that you are lucid dreaming will wake you up. However, once you get past this stage, you will find it is not hard to direct your dream in whatever direction you wish.

For the purposes of this book, I will assume that you are lucid dreaming with the intention of spending time with Michael. Before attempting to contact him in this way, think about where you would like to meet him. Would you like to walk along a quiet beach with him? You might prefer a woodland setting, or perhaps choose a gently flowing stream or a mountain peak offering breathtaking views. You could choose your livingroom or workplace, if you like. It does not matter where you choose, but it is a good idea to decide ahead of time, so that you and Michael meet in a place that is comfortable for you.

Consider the questions that you wish to ask Michael. Again, it is better to think about this beforehand, so that you will not waste any time.

Once you become aware that you are lucid dreaming, think of your need to communicate with Michael. You may find yourself instantly in his presence. However, you may feel as if you are flying for a few seconds before you find yourself with him.

After you have asked your questions and listened to the replies, ask Michael for any further advice he can give you. Thank him for his time and guidance, and then say goodbye. Usually, your dream will end at this point and you will drift into a deep sleep. Occasionally, you will be able to direct your dream elsewhere, and when this happens, I picture myself sleeping soundly, and within a minute or so, that is what happens.

When you wake up in the morning, spend a few minutes reliving the dream before you get out of bed. Record everything that you remember in your dream diary, and add any details that may come into your conscious mind later.

Dreams provide a vital link to our inner selves. Working with our dreams is useful on many levels. It aids self-understanding and acceptance. Dreams assist us to reach our full potential. They also allow us to communicate with the divine.

One hundred and fifty years ago, in *Walden; Or, Life in the Woods* (1854), Henry David Thoreau (1817–62) wrote: "If one advances confidently in the direction of his dreams, and endeavors to live the life which he has imagined, he will meet with a success unexpected in common hours."

Ten

HOW TO INTRODUCE MICHAEL TO OTHERS

M OST people start working with the archangels on their own. Something creates an initial interest in the subject, and the person finds him- or herself led into an exciting world of new discoveries and experience. It is natural to want to share the excitement of these findings with others. However, as everyone is different, you will find some people are receptive, while others may be totally opposed to your new interest. It can be disappointing when someone you care for is not interested in something that is of vital importance to you. However, there is nothing to be gained by trying to force them to your way of thinking.

It is much better to agree to disagree, and let them gradually become intrigued when they start to notice beneficial changes happening to you. Even then, it is better to err on the side of caution. Answer their questions, of course, and explain why you are doing certain things, but do not appear overly eager to interest them in what you are doing. Your answers to their questions might satisfy them, and be all they want to know. However, if they continue to ask questions, answer them to the best of your ability and suggest places, such as bookstores and the Internet, where they can find more information.

You are bound to come across some people who will think that you are doing the devil's work, and are well on your way to perdition. I have found from experience that these people will not listen to your point of view, and are interested only in pushing their particular beliefs down your throat. As it is impossible to have a rational discussion on this basis, it is better not to enter into a conversation that will end in an argument. Be gentle with these people. They genuinely believe that they are doing the right thing.

Hopefully, you will find someone who is just as interested as you are, and you will be able to further your explorations together. Many of the rituals in this book can be performed with two or more people. The results are frequently astounding. Much of what I do is on my own, but I've always noticed that when I'm conducting a ritual with other people, the results are more pronounced and dramatic. Consequently, I'm convinced that one plus one frequently equals three, four, and sometimes even five.

Many years ago, I had to be careful what I said in public, because there wasn't the same acceptance of the New Age that there is today. Nowadays, I can speak freely, and this often gives me a chance to introduce other people to the angelic kingdom.

Not long ago, I happened to meet a friend at a park before a summer concert. We had arrived early to get good seats, and he and his family had done the same. The subject came around to angels, and his wife mentioned that she was working with Raphael, because she needed some healing. The people sitting on both sides of us joined the conversation, and I had the opportunity to introduce several people to a subject they may not have considered before.

I don't regard such situations as coincidences. Usually, the people I speak to are ready to be introduced to the angelic kingdom, and I just happen to be the catalyst that prompts them to take the subject further. You will find the same thing happening to you as you continue your own explorations. If my friend had not broached the subject, I probably would not have spoken about it and the other people might still not know anything about it. Of course, if the subject had not interested them, they would not have joined into the conversation either. I believe that they were ready to learn, and that it was serendipitous that they happened to sit down next to us.

Sometimes, the subject will come around to angels while I am conducting a class on a totally different subject. In this situation, I will happily talk about angels if it feels right. Again, this sometimes introduces people to a subject they had not thought about before.

Some years ago, I flew from Los Angeles to Toronto, and the long flight was a pleasant one because the lady next to me and I talked about angels almost all the way. I cannot recall how the subject came up, but we enjoyed a fascinating conversation, and we both learned from it.

You will be able to help many people with your knowledge of angels and archangels. There will be a tendency to want to talk about them to everyone. Resist this, but be alert for opportunities to discuss them with people who are seriously interested and can benefit from the information. You will be amazed at the number of opportunities you will receive to talk about angels with others. This is a good example of the universe at work.

Eleven

HOW TO FIND THE MICHAEL INSIDE OF YOU

SOMETIMES people laugh when I suggest that they search for Michael inside themselves. They picture the physical Michael, but do not consider the various attributes of Michael that they already possess.

Michael is the archangel of courage, strength, truth, integrity, and protection. Whether you realize it or not, you already have all of these qualities in your makeup. Of course, some of them might be latent, and Michael is willing to help you work on any quality that is deficient. All you have to do is ask.

There is no need to wait until you require a specific quality. Obviously, it is better to develop courage and strength before you find yourself in an emotionally draining situation, as you will be able to handle the situation with less stress and discomfort.

However, it is never too late to ask Michael for help. Adelina, a woman I worked with many years ago, was a chronic liar. She would lie even when there was no need to. She was an attractive, likable person with a great sense of fun. However, few of her friendships lasted, as people tended to avoid her once they discovered that she seldom told the truth. Of course, on the few instances when she did tell the truth, no one believed her anyway, as they expected her to lie. It was a strange situation, and eventually Adelina told me that she lied in an attempt to boost her popularity. Of course, the result was the exact opposite.

Finally, Adelina decided to do something about this problem. A friend loaned her a book about angels, and she started asking Michael to help her become truthful and honest. Naturally, Adelina experienced a large number of problems as she gradually changed. Because people expected Adelina to lie, they found it disconcerting when she started telling the truth. On a number of occasions, she almost gave up. Fortunately, Michael helped her to transform her life.

"If he hadn't been beside me every time I was tempted to lie," she said, "I'd have gone straight back to my old ways. I probably hurt a lot of people by suddenly becoming too honest, but at last, finally, I was able to feel proud of myself. It was a difficult process, but now I know, without a shadow of doubt, that I can do anything. Michael is with me whenever I need him."

As well as helping you gain qualities that you lack, Michael can help you deal with negative aspects of your personality. Obviously, you have to know what these are before asking Michael for help. You will be aware of some of your less pleasing traits, but may not be aware of others. If necessary, ask someone you can trust to tell you what your negative traits are. It is important that you do not react aggressively or angrily to what you hear. The person is doing you a favor, and whether or not you agree with what you are told, it is information that you should think about afterward. If, for instance, you hear that you are proud, selfish, and egocentric, take some time to think about why the person you trusted told you these things, if they were not true. You may find, on reflection, that you do exhibit at least some of these qualities. Once you realize this, you can do something about them. Ask Michael to help you overcome the negative aspects of your nature, and be patient as Michael helps you gradually turn the negative aspects around.

Nathaniel is someone I have known for most of my life. We have never been close friends, but our paths cross occasionally. He is gregarious and outgoing, and I enjoy spending time with him every now and again. However, I prefer to meet him either at his home or mine, as he is incredibly rude and obnoxious to restaurant wait staff. His overbearing manner was unpleasant and unnecessary, yet he seemed totally unaware of it. Consequently, I was a little nervous when I met him some months ago at a large restaurant. I need not have been, as he was pleasant and charming with the servers. The change was so pronounced that I asked him what had happened.

He explained that one night his wife had refused to go out to dinner with him, as she was constantly mortified by his behavior. Nathaniel denied ever causing problems, and after an argument with his wife, went out for dinner with their friends, leaving her at home. For the first time in his life, he observed how he behaved during the course of the evening, and was shocked by what he saw. He returned home and apologized to his wife.

"And that's what caused this change in you?" I asked.

Nathaniel looked embarrassed, but then he laughed. "I can talk about this with you, but not too many other people. Margot got me to contact an angel. Michael, it was. I had to sit down and watch her light candles and say some prayers. I was just going along with it, to humor her, but suddenly I knew Michael was there. I couldn't see him, but it was this sudden sense of knowing that he was with us in the room. It sent a tingle right up my spine. I don't mind telling you that I cried. It was a highly emotional experience. After the first time, I asked Margot to do it again, and then we started working on my problems. We still are, as a matter of fact." Nathaniel shrugged. "I guess I have more hang-ups than most."

Nathaniel still has a long way to go, but thanks to Michael, is now on track. Instead of worrying about meeting him in public, I now look forward to spending time with him and hearing about how he is doing.

One approach to difficulties that I have found helpful is to ask Michael to walk beside me for just one day, while I focus on making a slight improvement in an area that has been causing me difficulty. At the end of the day I evaluate my progress. Invariably, I will be further ahead than I would have been without Michael's help. Naturally, once I see what has been achieved in just one day, I can then progress faster and further in the following days.

Another method is to relax and think about your problems. When you feel ready, invite Michael to join you and discuss what you could do to resolve them. This conversation should be a pleasant discussion between two close friends. There is no need to bemoan your fate or feel sorry for yourself. Michael is there to help you find a way to gain the qualities you feel you lack, and you should feel positive, rather than negative, about the outcome.

I have met people who felt they were so bad that they were beyond help. All of us contain good and bad qualities, and I have yet to meet someone who is beyond redemption. No matter what your past may have been like, you can turn your life around and become the person you want to be, by finding the Michael inside you.

A third method is to follow one of the rituals we have already covered, and use it to help you discover the Michael inside. Alternatively, you might like to use this method when relaxing or meditating. Once you are sufficiently relaxed, simply ask Michael to help you develop the qualities that you feel are lacking in your makeup. Often, you will sense the changes happening inside you, even while you are still talking with Michael.

No matter which method you use to find the Michael inside you, you will notice improvements almost immediately. Whenever you find yourself in a situation involving the qualities that Michael provides, remind yourself that

Michael is with you, and you will instantly experience a sense of quiet confidence and strength.

With Michael's help, there is no limit to how far you can go.

Twelve

CONCLUSION

I HOPE this book has helped you to gain contact with Michael so that you can experience the benefits of his love, comfort, and assistance in your life. I also hope it will encourage you to learn more about the other archangels and the entire angelic kingdom.

With the help of Michael and the other angels, you will be able to grow and develop into your full potential. You will discover your life's purpose. You will become more in touch with your divine nature. Every aspect of your life will expand as you open your mind and heart to the angelic realms.

I wish you enormous joy and happiness in your quest.

Notes

Introduction

1. John of Damascus, "Exposition of the Orthodox Faith," Book 2, translated by the Rev. S. D. F. Salmond, Principal of the Free Church College, Aberdeen, 1898. Published in *Post Nicene Fathers,* Schaff edition, Volume IX, Series 2. Also available online at: http://www.balamand.edu.lb/theology/WritingsSJD.htm

2. Examples include: Daniel 8:17, Daniel 10:11, Matthew 28:5, Mark 16:6, Luke 1:12–13, Luke 2:9, Acts 10:4.

3. Paul Roland. *Angels: An Introduction to Angelic Guidance, Inspiration and Love* (London, UK: Judy Piatkus (Publishers) Limited, 1999), 12.

4. Zecharia Sitchin. *Divine Encounters: A Guide to Visions, Angels, and Other Emissaries* (New York, NY: Avon Books, 1996), 261–262.

5. H. L. Pass. "Demons and Spirits." Article in *Encyclopae-dia of Religion and Ethics,* edited by J. Hastings (New York, NY: Charles Scribners, 1911), 583.

6. S. G. F. Brandon. *Religion in Ancient History* (London, UK: George Allen and Unwin Limited, 1973), 368.

7. Pseudo-Dionysius (translated by Colm Luibheid). *Pseudo-Dionysius: The Complete Works* (Mahwah, NJ: Paulist Press, 1987), 188.

8. Hildegard of Bingen. *Book of Divine Works with Letters and Songs,* edited by M. Fox (Santa Fe, NM: Bear and Company, 1987), 180–181.

9. Jacob Boehme. *The Aurora,* translated by J. Sparrow (London, UK: John M. Watkins and James Clarke, 1960), 272.

10. Thomas Traherne. *Centuries of Meditations* (Edin-burgh, Scotland: McInnes and Company, 1889), 362.

11. Emmanuel Swedenborg. *Heaven and its Wonders and Hell,* translated by J. C. Ager (New York, NY: Sweden-borg Foundation, 1930), 130–134.

12. Charles Baudelaire. *Les Fleurs du mal* (Paris, France: Classiques Garnier, 1994). The poem "Orgueil" is on page 177.

13. Andrew Welburn. *Mani, the Angel and the Column of Glory: An Anthology of Manichean Texts* (Edinburgh, UK: Floris Books, 1998), 11.

14. Paul Rorem in the Preface to *Pseudo-Dionysius: The Complete Works* (Mahwah, NJ: Paulist Press, 1987), 1.

15. Hildegard of Bingen. *Scivius* III, 1.

16. For further information on the Enochian language and Dr. John Dee see: *The Queen's Conjuror: The Life and Magic of Dr. Dee* by Benjamin Woolley (London, UK: HarperCollins Publishers, 2001), and *Enochian Magic for Beginners* by Donald Tyson (St. Paul, MN: Llewellyn Publications, 1997).

17. James H. Hindes. "The Hierarchies." Article in *Angels and Mortals:Their Co-Creative Power,* compiled by Maria Parisen (Wheaton, IL: Quest Books, 1990), 118–119.

18. Billy Graham. *Angels: God's Secret Agents* (Dallas, TX: Word Publishing, 1975).

19. R. H. Charles, editor. *The Greek Versions of the Testaments of the Twelve Patriarchs.* Edited from Nine Mss. Together with the Variants of the Armenian and Slavonic Versions and some Hebrew Fragments. (Oxford, UK: Clarendon Press, 1908), 3:3–6.

20. Helmer Ringgren (translated by David Green), *Israelite Religion.* London, UK: S. P. C. K., 1966), 311.

21. "And these are the names of the holy angels who watch. Uriel, one of the holy angels, who is over the world and over Tartarus. Raphael, one of the holy angels, who is over the spirits of men. Raguel, one of

the holy angels, who takes vengeance on the world of the luminaries. Michael, one of the holy angels, to wit, he is set over the best part of mankind and over chaos. Saraqâêl, one of the holy angels, who is set over the spirits, who sin in the spirit. Gabriel, one of the holy angels, who is over Paradise and the serpents and the Cherubim. Remiel, one of the holy angels, whom God set over those who rise."—*The Book of Enoch,* I:XX, translated by R. H. Charles. *The Book of Enoch* (London, UK: Society for Promoting Christian Knowledge, 1921), 46.

22. Matthew Black, commentator and editor. *The Book of Enoch or 1 Enoch: A New English Edition* (Leiden, Netherlands: E. J. Brill, 1985), 199.

23. Amesha spentas are the six Beneficent Immortals in Zoroastrianism. They are the divine beings, or archangels, who were created by Ahura Mazddā, the Wise Lord, to help look after all creation. Three of them are male and three female, and each has a specific month, festival, and element. Some accounts claim that there are seven amesha spentas, as Ahura Mazddā is sometimes considered to be an archangel. (Geoffrey Parrinder. *Worship in the World's Religions* [London, UK: Faber and Faber Limited, 1966], 88.)

24. Helmer Ringgren. *Israelite Religion,* 312.

Chapter One

1. George W. MacRae and William R. Murdock, translators. *The Apocalypse of Paul.* In The Nag Hammadi Library in English, edited by James M. Robinson (San Francisco, CA: Harper and Row, Inc., 1988), 256–259. The Apocalypse of Paul was probably written in Greek shortly before 400 C.E., and is the largest and possibly most influential of the many apocalyptic works that appeared around this time.

2. *The Greek Apocalypse of Baruch* is available in several translations, including two excellent ones by H. Maldwyn Hughes and A. W. Argyle. The most accessible translation is *The Greek Apocalypse of Baruch* (3 Baruch) in *Hellenistic Judaism and Early Christianity* by Daniel C. Harlow (Leiden, Netherlands: E. J. Brill, 1996).

3. Brian E. Daley. *The Hope of the Early Church: A Handbook of Patristic Eschatology* (Cambridge, UK: Cambridge University Press, 1991), 123.

4. Matthew Bunson. *Angels A to Z* (New York, NY: Crown Publishers, Inc., 1996), 182.

5. *The Testament of Abraham,* 9:5–6A. There are several translations available. My copy is *The Testament of Abraham: The Greek Recensions,* edited by Michael E. Stone (Missoula, MT: Society of Biblical Literature, 1972). There are two different versions of *The Testament of Abraham,* known as A and B. Version A is the

longer of the two, and in this account Abraham is transported on a cherubim chariot. In version B he is taken for a tour on a cloud.

6. Nathaniel Lardner. *History of the Early Heretics* (London, UK, 1780). Nathaniel Lardner (1684–1768) died before finishing this book, and it was completed by John Hogg.

7. Anna Jameson. *Legends of the Madonna* (Boston, MA: Houghton Mifflin and Company, 1895), 140.

8. David Gittings. *Spiritual Pilgrimage* (Hereford, UK: New Editions, 1996), 102.

9. S. G. F. Brandon. *Religion in Ancient History* (London, UK: George Allen and Unwin Limited, 1973), 367.

10. David Keck. *Angels and Angelology in the Middle Ages* (New York, NY: Oxford University Press, 1998), 39.

11. Paola Giovetti. *Angels: The Role of Celestial Guardians and Beings of Light* (York Beach, ME: Samuel Weiser, Inc., 1993), 69. Originally published by Edizioni Mediterranee, Rome, Italy, 1989.

12. Paola Giovetti. *Angels: The Role of Celestial Guardians and Beings of Light*, 95–96.

13. Rabbi Nehunia ben haKana (attributed to). *The Bahir*, translated by Aryeh Kaplan (York Beach, ME: Samuel Weiser, Inc., 1979), 5, 97.

14. Louis Ginzberg. *The Legends of the Jews, Volume 1*, translated by Henrietta Szold (Philadelphia, PA: The Jewish Publication Society of America, 1909), 384–388.

15. James Redfield, Michael Murphy and Sylvia Timbers. *God and the Evolving Universe* (New York, NY: Jeremy P. Tarcher/Putnam, 2002), 196.

16. Shaykh Muhammad Hisham Kabbani. *Angels Unveiled: A Sufi Perspective* (Chicago, IL: KAZI Publications, Inc., 1995), 170.

17. Shaykh Muhammad Hisham Kabbani. *Angels Unveiled: A Sufi Perspective,* 173.

18. Stephen Herbert Langdon. *The Mythology of all Races, Volume V: Semitic* (New York, NY: Cooper Square Publishers, Inc., 1964), 338–339.

19. Stephen Herbert Langdon. *The Mythology of all Races, Volume V: Semitic,* 363.

20. Anna Jameson. *Sacred and Legendary Art, Volume 1* (Boston, MA: Houghton Mifflin and Company, 1895), 87.

21. H. C. Moolenburgh, translated by Amina Marix-Evans. *A Handbook of Angels* (Saffron Walden, UK: The C. W. Daniel Company Limited, 1984), 99–100. Originally published 1984 by Uitgeverij Ankh-Hermes, Netherlands, as *Engelen*.

Chapter Two

1. Richard Webster. *Omens, Oghams and Oracles* (St. Paul, MN: Llewellyn Publications, 1995), 39–41.

2. Cornelia M. Parkinson. *Gem Magic* (New York, NY: Fawcett Columbine, 1988), 47.

3. Further information on the pendulum can be found in: Richard Webster, *Pendulum Magic for Beginners* (St. Paul, MN: Llewellyn Publications, 2002).

4. Migene González-Wippler. *Return of the Angels* (St. Paul, MN: Llewellyn Publications, 1999), 257.

5. Ken Ring. *Super Tramp* (Auckland, NZ: Milton Press, 1999), 251.

Chapter Seven

1. Brett Bravo. *Crystal Healing Secrets* (New York, NY: Warner Books, Inc., 1988), 24.

2. Louis Ginzberg. *The Legends of the Jews, Volume 1*, translated by Henrietta Szold, 300.

3. Shaykh Muhammad Hisham Kabbani. *Angels Unveiled: A Sufi Perspective*, 171.

4. Cornelia M. Parkinson. *Gem Magic* (New York, NY: Fawcett Columbine, 1988), 47.

Chapter Nine

1. Tara Ward. *Meditation and Dreamwork* (London, UK: Arcturus Publishing Limited, 2001), 249.

2. John Chrysostum. *Homilies on Matthew*, IV No. 18, v. 5.

3. Origen. *Against Celsus*, VI, 21–23.

4. Augustine Fitzgerald, *The Essays and Hymns of Synesius of Cyrene* (London, UK: Oxford University Press, 1930), 345.

5. For further information on this, see: Morton Kelsey. *Gods, Dreams and Revelation* (Minneapolis, MN: Augsburg Publishing House, 1968) and John A. Sanford, *Dreams: God's Forgotten Language* (New York, NY: Lippincott and Company, 1968).

6. Walter Franklin Price. *Noted Witnesses for Psychic Occurrences* (New Hyde Park, NY: University Books, Inc., 1963), 157. Originally published by the Boston Society for Psychic Research, 1928.

7. John Travers. *Dreamworking* (London, UK: G. Child and Company, Limited, 1978), 243.

8. Jayne Gackenbach and Jane Bosveld. *Control Your Dreams* (New York, NY: Harper & Row, Publishers, Inc., 1989), 166–167.

Suggested Reading

Apocrypha: The Books called Apocrypha according to the Authorized Version. London, UK: Oxford University Press, n.d.

Auerbach, Loyd. *Psychic Dreaming: A Parapsychologist's Handbook.* New York, NY: Warner Books, Inc., 1991.

Black, Matthew, commentator and editor. *The Book of Enoch or 1 Enoch: A New English Edition.* Leiden, Netherlands: E. J. Brill, 1985.

Brandon, S. G. F. *Religion in Ancient History.* London, UK: George Allen and Unwin Limited, 1973.

Brockington, L. H. *A Critical Introduction to the Apocrypha.* London, UK: Gerald Duckworth and Company Limited, 1961.

Bunson, Matthew. *Angels A to Z*. New York, NY: Crown Trade Paperbacks, 1996.

Burnham, Sophy. *A Book of Angels: Reflections on Angels Past and Present and True Stories of How They Touch Our Lives*. New York, NY: Ballantine Books, 1990.

Cahill, Thomas. *Desire of the Everlasting Hills*. New York, NY: Nan A. Talese, division of Doubleday Dell Publishing Group, Inc., 1999.

Connell, Janice T. *Angel Power*. New York, NY: Ballantine Books, 1995.

Daley, Brian E. *The Hope of the Early Church: A Handbook of Patristic Eschatology*. Cambridge, UK: Cambridge University Press, 1991.

Davidson, Gustav. *A Dictionary of Angels*. New York, NY: The Free Press, 1967.

Fox, Matthew and Rupert Sheldrake. *The Physics of Angels: Exploring the Realm Where Science and Spirit Meet*. San Francisco, CA: HarperSanFrancisco, 1996.

Gackenbach, Jayne and Jane Bosveld. *Control Your Dreams*. New York, NY: Harper and Row, Publishers, Inc., 1989.

Ginzberg, Louis, translated by Henrietta Szold. *The Legends of the Jews* (7 volumes). Philadelphia, PA: The Jewish Publication Society of America, 1909–1937.

Giovetti, Paola, translated by Toby McCormick. *Angels: The Role of Celestial Guardians and Beings of Light.* York Beach, ME: Samuel Weiser, Inc.,1993.

Hodson, Geoffrey. *The Angelic Hosts.* London, UK: The Theosophical Publishing House Limited, 1928.

Jones, Timothy. *Celebration of Angels.* Nashville, TN: Thomas Nelson Publishers, 1994.

Kabbani, Shaykh Muhammad Hisham. *Angels Unveiled: A Sufi Perspective.* Chicago, IL: KAZI Publications, Inc., 1995.

Milik, J. T. , editor. *The Books of Enoch: Aramaic Fragments of Qumrân Cave 4.* Oxford, UK: Oxford University Press, 1976.

Moolenburgh, H. C., translated by Amina Marix-Evans. *A Handbook of Angels.* Saffron Walden, UK: The C. W. Daniel Company Limited, 1984. Originally published as *Engelen* by Uitgeverij Ankh-Hermes, Netherlands, 1984.

Myer, Isaac. *Qabbalah, the Philosophical Writings of Solomon Ben Yehudah Ibn Gebirol or Avicebron.* London, UK: Robinson and Watkins, 1972. First published in Philadelphia, 1888.

Parrinder, Geoffrey. *Worship in the World's Religions.* London, UK: Faber and Faber Limited, 1961.

Pseudo-Dionysius, translated by Colm Luibheid. *Pseudo-Dionysius: The Complete Works*. Mahwah, NJ: Paulist Press, 1987.

RavenWolf, Silver. *Angels: Companions in Magic*. St. Paul, MN: Llewellyn Publications, 1996.

Ringgren, Helmer, translated by David Green. *Israelite Religion*. London, UK: S. P. C. K., 1966.

Shinners, John, editor. *Medieval Popular Religion 1000–1500: A Reader*. Peterborough, Canada: Broadview Press, 1997.

Swedenborg, Emmanuel, translated by George F. Dole. *Heaven and Hell*. West Chester, PA: Swedenborg Foundation, 1976.

Sweetman, J. Windrow. *Islam and Christian Theology* (4 volumes). London, UK: Lutterworth Press, 1947.

Tyson, Donald. *Enochian Magic for Beginners*. St. Paul, MN: Llewellyn Publications, 1997.

Webster, Richard. *Spirit Guides and Angel Guardians*. St. Paul, MN: Llewellyn Publications, 1998.

Welburn, Andrew. *Mani, the Angel and the Column of Glory: An Anthology of Manichaean Texts*. Edinburgh, Scotland: Floris Books, 1998.

Index

Aaron, 99

Abraham, 5–6, 100, 127, 149–150

Acherusian Lake, 4

Air (element), 29–30, 32, 44–45, 73–75, 92, 104, 115

Al-Taum, 16

altar, angelic, 9, 25–27, 35–36, 40, 66, 75, 77–78, 80, 82–83, 85, 89, 101, 105–106, 112

Amesha Spentas, xxii, 148

amethyst, 100–101, 110

angel(s), *see also* archangel(s), xi–xxii, 2, 5, 7, 9, 11–18, 22, 25, 27, 30, 33, 41, 49–50, 55, 61, 68, 71, 73, 80–81, 100–102, 113, 120, 122, 135–136, 138, 140, 143

Anthroposophical Society, xviii

Apsaras, xii

aquamarine, 33, 101, 103, 110

Free Magazine

Read unique articles by Llewellyn authors, recommendations by experts, and information on new releases. To receive a **free** copy of Llewellyn's consumer magazine, *New Worlds of Mind & Spirit,* simply call 1-877-NEW-WRLD or visit our website at www.llewellyn.com and click on *New Worlds.*

☾ LLEWELLYN ORDERING INFORMATION

Order Online:
Visit our website at www.llewellyn.com, select your books, and order them on our secure server.

Order by Phone:
- Call toll-free within the U.S. at 1-877-NEW-WRLD (1-877-639-9753). Call toll-free within Canada at 1-866-NEW-WRLD (1-866-639-9753)
- We accept VISA, MasterCard, and American Express

Order by Mail:
Send the full price of your order (MN residents add 7% sales tax) in U.S. funds, plus postage & handling to:
Llewellyn Worldwide
P.O. Box 64383, Dept. 0-7387-0540-3
St. Paul, MN 55164-0383, U.S.A.

Postage & Handling:

Standard (U.S., Mexico, & Canada). If your order is:
$49.99 and under, add $3.00
$50.00 and over, FREE STANDARD SHIPPING

AK, HI, PR: $15.00 for one book plus $1.00 for each additional book.

International Orders (airmail only):
$16.00 for one book plus $3.00 for each additional book

Orders are processed within 2 business days.
Please allow for normal shipping time. Postage and handling rates subject to change.

ARCHANGEL POSTER OFFER

MIGUEL   MICHAEL   מיכאל

Painting by Neal Armstrong for & Llewellyn Worldwide Publications

Grace your wall with an inspiring and beautiful archangel poster

Considered the most powerful angel
in the Christian, Judaic, and Islamic traditions,
Michael is protector, messenger, warrior, and healer.

Posters are 16 x 20 inches,
on high quality paper with a glossy finish

$9.95 each

How to Order:
Visit our website at www.llewellyn.com
Or order by phone, toll-free within the U.S.
1-877-NEW-WRLD (1-877-639-9753)
Price subject to change without notice

Spirit Guides &
Angel Guardians
Contact Your Invisible Helpers

Richard Webster

They come to our aid when we least expect it, and they disappear as soon as their work is done. Invisible helpers are available to all of us; in fact, we all regularly receive messages from our guardian angels and spirit guides but usually fail to recognize them. This book will help you to realize when this occurs. And when you carry out the exercises provided, you will be able to communicate freely with both your guardian angels and spirit guides.

You will see your spiritual and personal growth take a huge leap forward as soon as you welcome your angels and guides into your life. This book contains numerous case studies that show how angels have touched the lives of others, just like yourself. Experience more fun, happiness, and fulfillment than ever before. Other people will also notice the difference as you become calmer, more relaxed, and more loving than ever before.

1-56718-795-1, 368 pp., $5\,{}^{3}\!/_{16}$ x 8   **$9.95**

Spanish edition
Ángeles guardianes y guías espirituales
1-56718-786-2, 336 pp., $5\,{}^{3}\!/_{16}$ x 8, illus.   **$12.95**

To order by phone, call 1-877-NEW-WRLD
Prices subject to change without notice